DATE			

Memphis Since Crump

Memphis

KNOXVILLE

Since Crump

Bossism, Blacks, and Civic Reformers

1948–1968   *by David M. Tucker*

THE UNIVERSITY OF TENNESSEE PRESS

Library of Congress Cataloging in Publication Data

Tucker, David M   1937–
  Memphis Since Crump.

  Bibliography: p.
  Includes index.
  1. Memphis—Politics and government.
2. Afro-Americans—Tennessee—Memphis—Politics and
suffrage. 3. Urban renewal—Tennessee—Memphis.
I. Title.
JS1092.T8   320.9′768′19   79-12211
ISBN 0-87049-282-9

The City

Not by her houses neat
Nor by her well-built walls
Not yet again
Neither by dock nor street
A city stands or falls
But by her men.

Not by the joiner's skill,
Nor work in wood or stone,
Comes good to her or ill,
But by her men alone.

—ALCAEUS
Inscription on marble walls of Memphis City Hall

Contents

Illustrations

Preface

This is a study of race and metropolitan politics in twentieth century
Memphis. It began as the story of those civic reformers who led the
second urban renaissance (1948–1968) in Memphis, but an investigation of recent politics in a major city must recognize the central
role of race. Black voters were as essential to the long rule of the local
Crump political machine as they were to the later victory of civic reform. Boss Crump had ruled the black community by the old machine tactics of patronage, persuasion, and fear. The civic reformers
who rose to power in the 1950s discarded the old methods; instead,
they invited blacks to join their civic reform organizations and share
their faith in good government and urban renewal. For a time blacks
and white reformers worked together, but blacks grew tired of white
moderation and deserted the civic reformers to pursue ethnic goals
of their own community, beginning a racial separatism in politics
that undermined civic reform and led to a racially divided city. The
politics of race displaced the politics of reform in Memphis.

   The story of reform begins with Boss Crump's absolutism, which
so rubbed and chafed a few sensitive white Memphians that they angrily organized a civic reform movement that proved vigorous
enough to last two decades. Their concerns had at first been more
international than local. Deeply influenced by Cold War fears, they

had embraced world government as the sole means for preserving Western democracy and were advocates of Federal Union; in fact, they were successful in making the idea a matter of national political debate. They had enlisted the support of Representative Estes Kefauver and begun promoting his election to the United States Senate when they ran into Crump's opposition. The movement to save democracy in the West became a campaign for democracy in Memphis.

The seven upper-class whites who launched the Federal Union campaign were joined by a CIO leader attracted by the candidate's support of labor unions and a black insurance executive interested in Kefauver's support of civil rights. These different Memphians became a firm coalition closely united by Crump's attacks, sharing a common belief in democratic principles, which they understood as equal opportunity for the individual to develop his abilities, make his own decisions, and control his own future. Their shared faith and their alliance would provide a dynamic local municipal reform, the beginning of peaceful desegregation, and a liberal Democratic politics in state and national elections.

Following the 1948 election of Kefauver to the United States Senate, the reformers organized the Civic Research Committee to work for honest elections and the good local government advocated by the National Municipal League. Although they had helped to break Crump's control over state-wide elections, they remained unable to defeat the machine locally until after Mr. Crump died in 1954. They then elected the leader of their coalition, Edmund Orgill, to become mayor of Memphis, but they failed to achieve an ideal reform administration because Crumpites still held most of the seats on the city commission.

The coalition extended itself to the black community until 1959, when Mayor Orgill retired, younger blacks entered their own political ticket, and reformers' hopes for greater political power led them to separate their concern for blacks from their political campaigns. They organized the Memphis Committee on Community Relations to correct black grievances and the Citizens Association for winning white votes and pushing good government reforms. Without black support, the white reformers elected candidates pledged to metropolitan consolidation and council-manager government. The old city commission charter was replaced, but then the rise of conservative white Republicanism and black political separatism splintered the community and deprived the liberal reformers of all political power and influence.

The coalition's story is one of leadership and failure in the nation's seventeenth largest city. Men of integrity, competence, and compassion did emerge to restore local democracy, enact reforms for good government, and work for bi-racial cooperation until racial polarization eliminated reformers from leadership and produced a local civic distress that grew in severity and became national with the assassination of Reverend Martin Luther King, Jr.

Acknowledgments

The reformers welcomed historians to study their record. Having nothing to conceal—unlike Mr. Crump—they opened their archives for all scholars. Edmund Orgill, the reform leader, made this study possible by placing his personal papers, those of Edward J. Meeman, the Civic Research Committee, and the Citizens Association in the Memphis State Library. Orgill and the other "good government volunteers" also cheerfully answered a historian's questions and read early drafts of the manuscript. John W. Spence, a political scientist and a former reporter for the *Memphis Press-Scimitar*, insisted that I interview a few Crumpites but also reinforced my regard for the civic leaders who pursued good government for their community rather than for personal power. Professor Lee S. Greene, who wrote much of the new Memphis city charter, sought to moderate my criticism of Boss Crump and to correct my understanding of Tennessee politics. Zane L. Miller persuaded me that the Memphis story should not be viewed simply as the opposition of boss and reformers but as a study of race and metropolitan politics in a city by no means unique nor peculiarly Southern. Thomas W. Collins provided information about local garbage collectors; Melvin C. Barber III constructed the black/white map of Memphis; Nancy Hurley

shared her perceptive criticism of the text; and Eleanor McKay provided access to the Mississippi Valley Collection of photographs
from the *Commercial Appeal.*

Memphis Since Crump

1.

The City Where King Was Killed

If Martin Luther King, Jr. had sought a typical American city in which to end his civil rights career, he could have selected none more representative than Memphis, which, despite Southern white efforts to keep it down in Dixie, had never really been peculiarly Southern. The river town stands halfway between St. Louis and New Orleans, perched high on a bluff overlooking the Mississippi River flood plain. The "mid-America city," as the local chamber of commerce would call it, had been a border town, unable to be completely a Southern city even in the old days of racial discrimination. Even during the years of disfranchisement, Memphis, unlike Atlanta, New Orleans, or Dallas, never took the vote from blacks who participated in its urban game of politics. There were no white party primaries in Memphis.

Memphis developed a black community years before most Northern cities. More than a hundred years ago the migration of rural Negroes made Memphis 40 percent black. It all began in the second year of the Civil War, when invading Union Armies established a freedmen's camp south of the river town for escaping plantation slaves. Most of the freedmen stayed on after the war, swelling the black population from four thousand to fifteen thousand. They joined in the urban game of ethnic politics, which had already

3

elected an Irishman mayor of Memphis, winning seats on the city council. By 1875 an ethnic coalition of blacks, Irish, and Italians had captured city hall completely from the Anglo-Southerners, with the black share six seats on the council and the important wharf-master post for Ed Shaw. These black politicians certainly refused to conform to the Sambo or Hambone stereotype held by Southern whites. Shaw, a product of the Ohio Valley, spoke a Northern white English, ran a saloon and gambling place on Linden, and came out forcefully for public school integration, declaring: "When the Irish-man or the German comes to this country, his children are admitted to the schools the very day after they land, while the children of us native Americans are not allowed to enter them, but are set apart, are tabooed and ostracized."[1]

Black protest leadership failed to secure desegregation of the schools. With the erosion of Northern Republican support for civil rights, Memphis blacks turned from the militancy of Shaw to the accommodating fraternal leadership that sought reconciliation with the local white economic establishment. Gathering behind the lead-ership of Hezekiah Henley, a blacksmith and the president of the local Independent Order of Pole-Bearers, the black community acted out its reconciliation with the Southern white man in a public Fifth of July celebration in 1875. On a speaker's platform at the city fair grounds, the wall of hostility was breached when pretty, light-brown Miss Lou Lewis presented a bouquet of flowers to Confederate cav-alry General Nathan Bedford Forrest, a former slave trader and head of the Ku Klux Klan. Receiving the flowers with a bow, Gen-eral Forrest said, "Miss Lewis, ladies and gentlemen—I accept these flowers as a token of reconciliation between the white and colored races of the South." He went on to say that he had been maligned and misunderstood by the black race. He was their friend and would help them whenever he could. "I want to elevate every man, and to see you take your places in your shops, stores, and offices," Forrest said. "I assure you that every man who was in the Confederate Army

1. *Memphis Daily Appeal,* June 28, 1872; David M. Tucker, "Black Politics in Memphis, 1865–1875," *West Tennessee Historical Society Papers* 26 (1972), 13–19; Armstead L. Robinson, "Black Memphis, 1850–1870" (unpublished book manu-script).

is your friend. We were born on the same soil, breathe the same air, live on the same land, and why should we not be brothers and sisters."[2]

Although the drama at the fair grounds had been organized by blacks, a strong possibility exists that Hezekiah Henley had followed the suggestion of prominent white Memphians. Certainly Anglo-Southerners had much to gain by reconciliation and had expressed a desire to end racial hostilities. After the city election of 1874, one Southerner had informed the Memphis *Daily Appeal* that "in the last municipal election the Irish voter had exhibited no repugnance to 'clasp hands over the bloody chasm' with sambo, when an office was to be retained or obtained thereby. Then why should the American of the south longer hesitate to strengthen his power by an alliance with him? What Pat can do surely the late master can accomplish."[3] Perhaps the masters had been scheming with Hezekiah Henley before the celebration at the fair grounds; if so, it was a well-kept secret, but after July 5, Henley certainly had the enthusiastic support of local Democrats.

In the next municipal election, Hezekiah Henley led more than half of the black voters to abandon black candidates and vote the entire slate of Southern whites into office. The Democratic press was delighted. "The colored people of Memphis forever buried their antagonism to the whites," the Memphis *Appeal* announced. "They sank race prejudices in a noble desire to promote the great material interests of Memphis." The *Appeal* also noted the demise of Ed Shaw's leadership, quoting a black voter who had announced on election day: "Ed Shaw done popped de last whip ober dis chile: I dun cut loose now. . . ."[4]

Black Memphis voters ended their era of protest in this election of 1876, but while seeking peace and harmony with whites they were not abandoning hopes for equality and manhood. Neither Henley nor any other black leader suggested that his race should abandon their political rights, and the local white Democrats did not immediately seek to stop blacks from holding office. For another decade

2. *Daily Memphis Avalanche,* July 6, 1875; David M. Tucker, *Black Pastors and Leaders* (Memphis: Memphis State Univ. Press, 1975), 33.

3. *Memphis Daily Appeal,* Jan. 7, 1874.

4. *Ibid.,* Jan. 14, 15, 1876.

blacks were elected to city government and appointed to the police force, but then white racism severely restricted black political power. After 1886 no black could be elected to city office, and by the nineties Memphis witnessed its first lynchings.

An alarming deterioration of race relations developed during the late 1880s and early 1890s, not only in Memphis and across the South but even in the North, as the forces of reaction overturned civil rights, promoting racial segregation, disfranchisement, and even lynching. In the long struggle against lynching, a black Memphis woman, Ida B. Wells, deserves more credit than any other individual for having brought this practice before the eyes of the world and, in so doing, having accelerated the establishment of law and decency in the American South.[5]

Born in 1862, the daughter of house servants in Holly Springs, Mississippi, Miss Wells attended local Rust College and then, like thousands of other Mississippi Negroes, moved north to Memphis, the striving commercial center of the Mid-South. There she taught at Kortecht Public School and won applause for her vigorous protest against the new state railroad segregation law. She paid first class fare in order to assert her right to ride in the railroad's ladies' car; forced to leave, she fought to the point of taking the Chesapeake, Ohio, and Southwestern to court in 1884. She even won the local decision, although it was later reversed by the Supreme Court of Tennessee. After publishing an account of her struggles in the local black press, Miss Wells won such applause that she began to write regularly.

As a serious journalist, Miss Wells purchased a third interest in the local *Free Speech and Headlight,* which defended its black readers against the new white racism. In *Free Speech* she declared:

> The dailies of our city say that the whites must rule this country. But that is an expression without a thought. It must be borne in mind that the Lord is going to have something to say about this and all other government. It may be expected that the black man will press his claim "till Shiloh comes."

5. David M. Tucker, "Miss Ida B. Wells and Memphis Lynching," *Phylon* 32 (Summer 1971), 112–22; Alfreda M. Duster, ed. *Crusader for Justice: The Autobiography of Ida B. Wells* (Chicago: Univ. of Chicago Press, 1970).

The old southern voice that was once heard and made the Negroes jump and run like rats to their holes is "shut up," or might well be, for the Negro of today is not the same as Negroes were thirty years ago, and it can't be expected that the Negro of today will take what was forced upon him thirty years back. So it is no use to be talking now about Negroes ought to be kept at the bottom where God intended for them to stay; the Negro is not expected to stay at the bottom.[6]

It was Miss Wells' editorials against the Memphis lynchings of 1892 that first brought her to the national attention of white America. It all began in south Memphis, on the curve of Walker Avenue and Mississippi Boulevard, where a joint stock grocery store had been organized by black Memphians. The Peoples' Grocery Store, as it was called, entered competition with a white merchant, W. H. Barret, who operated a grocery just across the street. Relations between the two businesses were never friendly, and friction was eventually followed by physical violence. After several incidents, which Barret seems to have instigated himself, the white man persuaded a grand jury in Shelby County to indict the officials of Peoples' Grocery for maintaining a nuisance. Enraged, the black community held a meeting during which certain speakers reportedly called for cleaning out the "damned white trash" with dynamite. At this point Barret appealed to Shelby County's criminal court Judge Julius J. DuBose, charging his competitors with conspiring against whites and securing warrants for the arrest of two of them who had spoken out at the meeting. Barret, it seems, then had the Peoples' Grocery informed that a white mob was planning to assault the store. When nine deputy sheriffs dressed in civilian clothing converged on the grocery after dark in order to deliver their arrest warrants, they were taken for a mob and fired upon.[7]

After three deputies were shot down with head and face wounds, most of the blacks ran while the deputies rushed in and arrested Calvin McDowell, the grocery clerk, and Will Steward, a stockholder. The cry of race riot was given, and the whole of Memphis became a

6. *Memphis Weekly Avalanche,* July 13, 1889; no file of *Free Speech* survived, and only those items reprinted by the white press are available for historians.

7. The black account is supported by the white neighborhood meeting which held W. H. Barret to be a "bad citizen," *Weekly Appeal-Avalanche,* March 16, 1892.

walking arsenal. Armed white men and boys helped the deputies round up and arrest thirty more accused rioters, among them Tom Moss, the mail carrier and Methodist Sunday school teacher who served as president of the store. Not content with arresting all accused rioters, Judge DuBose took illegal action to disarm the black community and ordered the arms of the Tennessee Rifles, a Negro state militia company, to be confiscated. The black armory was forcibly entered and the rifles carried to the sheriff's office. When neither local authorities nor the state militia commander protested the breach of law, Negro officers chose to announce the disbandment of their company in a bitter press release: "To wear the livery of a commonwealth that regards us with distrust and suspicion, a commonwealth that extracts an oath from us to defend its laws and then fails to protect us in the rights it guarantees, is an insult to our intelligence and manhood."[8]

At three o'clock on Wednesday morning, four days after the shoot-out on the Curve, nine white men, apparently deputy sheriffs, entered the county jail, seized Tom Moss, Calvin McDowell, and Will Stewart, who were regarded as the leaders of the Peoples' Grocery, took the prisoners a mile north of the jail, and shot them in cold blood on a vacant lot next to the Chesapeake and Ohio tracks. Thus three men were lynched in a city of more than eighty-five thousand and without the remotest chance that the murderers would ever be brought to trial.

Appalled by this, the worst atrocity against blacks since the Memphis police riot of 1866, the black community turned out by the thousands for the largest funeral procession ever to have taken place in Memphis. Resolutions condemning the lynchings and recommending emigration were adopted at a black town meeting; and the cries of "On to Oklahoma," which had already been heard for several years, sent entire church congregations west, across the Mississippi, and over the Old Military Road. A few hundred black Memphians may have fled the city not only in search of freedom for their

8. Cleveland *Gazette,* April 2, 1892; Tucker, "Miss Ida B. Wells and Memphis Lynching," 116.

children, but with the vague hope that depopulating the area would cause the whites to regret their violent oppression of black people.[9]

In the weeks following the lynching, Miss Wells' angry editorials demanded the trial and conviction of the murderers. The journalist also took the train out to Oklahoma herself to assess the territorial advantages for future black immigration; and at home she participated in the black community's boycott of the Memphis streetcars. The first threats on Miss Wells' life, however, came only after an editorial in *Free Speech* on May 21, in which she disputed the old rationalization of the whites for lynching, intimating that Southern white women were sexually attracted to black men. In the article, which responded to the lynching of eight more Negroes across the South that week, Miss Wells dared to comment, "Nobody in this section of the country believes the old thread-bare lies that Negro men rape white women. If Southern white men are not careful they will over-reach themselves and public sentiment will have a reaction, or a conclusion will be reached which will be very damaging to the moral reputation of their women."[10]

At this, the Memphis *Scimitar,* assuming that the article was written by a man, threatened that, "unless the Negroes promptly applied the remedy it would be the duty of the whites to tie the author to a stake, brand him on the forehead and perform a surgical operation on him with a pair of shears." The Memphis *Commercial* agreed: "There are some things the Southern white man will not tolerate, and the obscene intimations of the foregoing have brought the writer to the outermost limit of public patience."[11] The white city leaders called an urgent meeting at the Merchants Exchange and voted to attempt to head off yet another lynching by sending a delegation to warn the *Free Speech* never to repeat such ideas or "suffer the consequences." Not surprisingly, editor Wells was not there to receive the committee, having chosen already to leave the Bluff City

9. Cleveland *Gazette,* April 2, May 28, 1892; Nashville *Daily American,* March 11, 1892.

10. Nashville *Daily American,* May 26, 1892; Tucker, "Miss Ida B. Wells and Memphis Lynching," 116.

11. Nashville *Daily American,* May 26, 1892.

for the relative safety of the North; and the Memphis sheriff put a final end to *Free Speech,* selling the newspaper office and paying off the creditors.[12]

Miss Wells joined the staff of the *New York Age* and launched the crusade against lynching that gained the nation's attention. Lynch law had reached its highest level in history, and Miss Wells determined to bring the matter before the public eye. Not content with merely telling her story in the Afro-American press, she sought to present her case before an international audience. When the British editor of *Anti-Caste* asked her to speak in England, Miss Wells departed for Britain immediately. The black American journalist had been invited by Catherine Impey, editor of *Anti-Caste* in Aberdeen, Scotland, who explained in a letter of March 1893: "We want you to come over and help us begin the organization of an anti-slavery movement."[13] Miss Impey, a reformer who hoped that lectures on lynching would arouse moral sentiment for racial equality in the American South and throughout the British empire, guaranteed that all of Miss Wells' expenses would be paid. The American journalist accepted the offer, began with a lecture in the Music Hall at Aberdeen, and told her story in more than a dozen cities in Scotland and England. Through lectures that were praised as lucid, cultured, and effective, Englishmen were given their first opportunity to hear and applaud the Afro-American opposition to lynch law. "Her quiet, refined manner," the *Manchester Guardian* observed, "her intelligence and earnestness, her avoidance of all oratorical tricks, and her dependence upon the simple eloquence of facts make her a powerful and convincing advocate. . . ."[14]

British audiences were so sympathetic that Miss Wells returned again the next spring for a longer trip, which she confined in the main to London. There she visited all the journals that influenced English opinion and spoke to more than a hundred nonconformist churches, clubs, drawing gatherings, and dinner parties. Among her successes was a large breakfast reception for members of Parliament and their wives at the Westminster Palace Hotel, where she in-

12. Kansas City *American Citizen,* July 1, 1892.
13. Topeka *Call,* April 15, 1893.
14. *Manchester Guardian,* May 9, 1893.

10

formed her audience of the increased frequency and barbarity of lynchings in the Southern states and the failure of either local officials or Northern opinion to insist that legal due process replace mob violence. Miss Wells then asked for and received the promise that English public opinion would endorse the basic right of a fair trial for every Southern Negro accused of a crime.

In speeches and in a pamphlet, *United States Atrocities* (London, 1893), Miss Wells indicted lynching as the latest attempt to preserve white supremacy at any cost. The American press and pulpit were afraid to resist lynching, she contended, because they had swallowed the Southern myths about black men raping white women. The chastity of white women was perfectly safe among black men, Miss Wells stressed: "White men lynch the offending Afro-American not because he is a despoiler of virtue, but because he succumbs to the smiles of white women." She supported her claim by presenting recent items from the press about white women in Memphis who had seduced or voluntarily submitted to black men. Further to discredit the Southern fiction that lynch law was only used to check the "bestial propensities of black men," she cited statistics from the *Chicago Tribune* showing that during the past nine months only one-third of the men who were lynched had even been charged with rape.

The newspaper woman made Memphis her prime target. Not only had she an account to settle with the white community there, but the city was an excellent example of the white South's barbarity in general. On July 22, 1893, three thousand Memphians watched as a Saturday night crowd broke into the Shelby County jail and seized Lee Walker, an accused rapist. The mob stripped the man of his clothing, cut his throat, hanged him on a telegraph pole outside the jail, and then burned his body, all without a shot ever being fired by Sheriff McLendon in defense of the prisoner. Nor would the lynchers ever be tried, for, as the *Appeal-Avalanche* argued, "Walker was guilty—not of murder, or arson or forgery, but of rape, a crime which, whenever and wherever committed, calls for reprisal at the hands of the citizenship of the particular community."[15] But even Memphis had her Achilles' heel, her fear for her reputation and

15. Memphis *Appeal-Avalanche,* July 23, 28, Aug. 3, 1893.

commercial prosperity; and to the horror of the city's merchants, Miss Wells went to work on this weak spot, holding up the Bluff City's sins for the world to view.

Lectures produced more than applause and petitions to the American ambassador; they won for Miss Wells special interviews with the British press. News clippings of these interviews soon flooded in through the mails, reaching the white Memphis press with letters that asked, for example, if the city were really as brutal and heartless as was suggested in the article, "The Bitter Cry of Black America—a New Uncle Tom's Cabin." The Memphis editors must have winced on discovering the articles that were published in the *London Sun:*

> Miss Ida B. Wells is a negress, a young lady of little more than twenty years of age, a graceful, sweet-faced, intelligent, courageous girl. She hails from Memphis, Tenn. She is not going back there just now, because the white people are anxious to hang her up by the neck in the market place, and burn the soles of her feet, and gouge her beautiful dark eyes out with red-hot irons. This is what the Southern American white man does with a Negro or negress for preference, when he wants a holiday sensation; and when he finds a charming victim, such as this sweet girl would make, the mayor of the town orders the schools to be closed, and the little scholars turn out in holiday ribbons, and their parents don the Sunday go-to-meeting best, and lead the youngsters out by the hand. They all go out to see the fun, and have their photographs taken at the scene of martyrdom, and there is much rejoicing over the black sinner that repenteth not.[16]

Miss Wells' lectures were a smashing success. For one thing, they inspired the English to form an anti-lynching league with a treasury of 5,000 pounds for the purpose of investigating and publicizing the persecution of Southern Negroes in America. Naturally the merchants back in Memphis were alarmed at the impact of Ida Wells' lectures: being among the largest cotton exporters in the world, they depended upon the English textile industry for much of their business. It was no surprise, then, that the capitalists of the Merchants Exchange who owned the local white press felt compelled to reprint certain British reports of Miss Wells' lectures abroad in order to re-

16. *London Sun* reprinted in Memphis *Appeal-Avalanche,* June 12, 1894.

fute their charges against the Bluff City. The Memphis *Commercial Appeal* accused her of gross exaggeration and insisted that Memphis was really a decent place for blacks to live. But significantly, in this effort to repair the city's damaged reputation, newspaper editors at last condemned lynching unequivocally and even tried to make their position retroactive by insisting that they had never approved mob law.

Influence is difficult to measure, to be sure; but when the Memphis lynching of 1894 occurred shortly after Miss Wells' return from England (six accused barn burners were shot while being brought to the Shelby County jail), white business leaders immediately took conspicuous steps to condemn the crime publicly. Businessmen called a public meeting in the Merchants Exchange, where they adopted resolutions censuring the "wicked, fiendish and inexcusable massacre," demanded the "arrest and conviction of the murderers," and raised one fund for apprehending "the criminials" and another for the benefit of the widows and orphans of the "murdered men." Never before had the white citizens made such a forthright condemnation of racial lynching. It was time indeed, the *Commercial Appeal* explained, to rise up in opposition to barbarism and murder because "if this crime goes unpunished," the paper warned, "every friend of Memphis must be dumb before the accusations of its enemies, for silence will be our only refuge from the pitiless fire of denunciation that will be heaped upon us."[17]

A Shelby County grand jury promptly indicted thirteen white men for murder, went on record as being appalled by the outrage, and announced their hope for conviction and the death penalty. "We cannot close this report," the grand jury said, "without expressing our horror of the cold-blooded, brutal butchery of these six defenseless men, the cruelty of which would cause even a savage to hang his head in shame." And although the city never succeeded in convicting the band of lynchers, the practical need to end lynching and the new philosophy which it forced on the city's leadership put an end to the crime in Memphis and even stopped talk of disfranchisement.[18]

17. Memphis *Commercial Appeal,* Sept. 8, 17, 1894.
18. Tucker, "Miss Ida B. Wells and Memphis Lynching," 122; more than 20 years later, in 1917, a final lynching did occur just outside the city limits; in 1891

While Miss Wells never returned, thousands of Mississippi blacks continued to move north to Memphis during the 1890s, swelling the black population to 49,910 and helping Memphis become the third Southern city to pass the 100,000 population mark. Memphis trailed only New Orleans and Baltimore in the South; in the North many cities were larger, but only Washington, D.C., New York, and Philadelphia included more black citizens in 1900.

Memphis attracted Mississippi blacks who were disfranchised by their state constitution. Rural laborers and the black bourgeoisie from Mississippi towns moved north for political freedom as well as the educational and economic opportunities of a city. Three-fourths of the incoming black immigrants were Mississippi-born, while the other fourth came from Arkansas, Louisiana, and Alabama. These immigrants would outnumber native Memphians. When the origins of black Memphians were analyzed in 1930, fewer than half of the 96,550 were found to be Tennessee natives.[19]

All the roads in the Mid-South led to Memphis, a bustling river town and the home of Beale Street. Many a black had taken a weekend excursion on the Yazoo and Mississippi Valley Railway to see the sights and pleasures of black Beale. There one could smell the barbecued pig, the hog snout restaurants, the chitterling and pig ear cafés. There were black saloons to see as well as Church Amusement Park, lawyers, doctors, druggists, newspapers and the impressive Beale Street Baptist Church. Beale was the black center for business, entertainment, vice, and religion.[20]

Black women from rural Mississippi came up to find work as cooks or washerwomen and to secure a public school education for their children. In addition to the usual domestic and yard jobs, black men found work as switchmen in the city railroad yards, which employed a thousand blacks, more than any other railway center in the nation. Lumber had become the city's major industry

---

Tennessee did adopt the Dortch law, requiring a secret ballot and a poll tax, a suffrage restriction that slightly reduced black voting in Memphis.

19. U.S. Bureau of the Census, *Negroes in the United States 1920–1930* (Washington: GPO, 1935), 33, 39.

20. George W. Lee, *Beale Street: Where the Blues Began* (New York: R.O. Ballou, 1934).

and source of employment for blacks. As the major hardwood producer in the world, Memphis thrived, with the raucous industry of thirty sawmills ripping and tearing the great logs that were floated in on the Mississippi. Sawed lumber for furniture went to Wisconsin and Michigan; material for wagons, buggies, and agricultural implements went by train to Illinois and Ohio factories; and Memphis had forty manufacturing plants of its own for turning the lumber into finished products. Skilled black workers in the cooperage plants cut oak staves that were loaded on barges and floated down the river, bound for Europe, where they were eventually turned into wine casks.[21]

While thousands of black men provided labor for the lumber industry, a smaller group worked as skilled craftsmen in the building industry. The American Federation of Labor locals forced most blacks into separate unions with lower wage scales, but despite union discrimination, hundreds of carpenters, brickmasons, plasterers, and painters found ready employment because the rapid growth of the city population created a demand for construction. These were good times even for black contractors, and a few such as J. W. Sanford grew wealthy.

In the black neighborhoods a small middle class competed for the ghetto business against the Italian merchant, who was "a good mixer and a great jollier."[22] Even though the grocery business had a history of black failures, more than fifty Negro merchants persistently tried to outsell the Italians. Blacks may have left dry goods to the Jews, but they managed their own restaurants, drugstores, laundries, and undertakers. There were even two black newspapers, although by far the most spectacular business success was in gambling, saloons, and prostitution, all of which the river town had quite willingly harbored since they helped to pay the enormous municipal debts that began in the 1870s after an epidemic of yellow fever depopulated

21. William D. Miller, *Memphis During the Progressive Era* (Memphis: Memphis State Univ. Press, 1957), 45-47; W. E. B. DuBois (ed.), *The Negro American Artisan* (Atlanta, Ga.: Atlanta Univ. Press, 1912), 46; *Commercial Appeal,* Aug. 20, 1905; Nov. 28, 1915.

22. G. P. Hamilton, *The Bright Side of Memphis* (Memphis: G. P. Hamilton, 1908), 17.

the city. Anyone, black or white, who brought money to the city treasury and paid monetary tribute to the politicians and the public charities was welcome and allowed to prosper. So it was, for example, that Robert R. Church, after opening his first saloon in the 1860s, had risen to the top of the economic ladder to become possibly the wealthiest Negro in America. After making his fortune, Church turned from the underworld to Beale Street banking. In 1906, after the Negro Business League urged black men to establish their own banks, Church joined a score of business and professional men to create the Solvent Savings Bank and Trust. This new venture in local black capitalism steadily gained the confidence and patronage of black people and four years later led other businessmen to organize a competitor. Illinois-born funeral directors J. Jay Scott and H. Wayman Wilkerson formed the Fraternal Savings Bank in 1910, giving the city two black banking establishments.[23]

In addition to the businessmen, a respectable brown professional class thrived on the fringes of the black community. Forty-one black physicians, seven dentists, and twelve attorneys cultivated a black society maintained by rigid discrimination, favoring the educated, light-complexioned, and well-mannered. Society had its dances, dinners, musical shows, and literary societies, and the sons and daughters of the social aristocrats exchanged formal printed invitations to their own exclusive parties. The social whirl of the Primrose Club and the Toxoway Tennis Club included hiring the Steamer Charles Organ for riverboat parties where W. C. Handy provided the sophisticated music for programmed dances.

The black middle class could also organize to make political demands. The Colored Citizens' Association sounded out mayoral candidates and put price tags on their endorsements. Blacks asked for a fair share of urban services—paved and lighted streets, neighborhood parks, Negro doctors to examine black schoolchildren, and one day a week for their children to visit the segregated city zoo. Black leaders were restrained in their demands, even though their community contributed one-fourth or more of the city ballots, since

23. David M. Tucker, *Lieutenant Lee of Beale Street* (Nashville: Vanderbilt Univ. Press, 1971), 14–17.

16

middle-class blacks actually controlled fewer black votes than did the saloonkeepers and ward bosses. The two-dollar poll tax kept many blacks from registering and allowed the Crump machine to register for them and cast their votes.[24]

Memphis, like other cities, developed a political machine headed by a boss who forged a coalition of the foreign born, the blacks, the business community, and the illicit underworld of vice.[25] The Memphis Boss had actually begun as a middle-class reformer from the Merchants Exchange who promised to bring business efficiency to city government. But once elected by the middle class in 1909, E. H. Crump's base of support shifted to ethnic and black wards.[26] The foreign-born were only 5 percent of the city population, but the black community added another 40 percent, and it was the most easily manipulated of all. With payoff money collected from saloons, gambling dives, and houses of prostitution, the Crump organization bought poll taxes and voted for thousands of citizens who never appeared at the polls. Crump's machine would never be beaten at the polls from 1909 until his death in 1954.

No black was ever slated for election to local office by the Crump machine. White racism plus a change made in 1909 in the city commission charter to require at-large elections prevented the election of any black, but the political organization never sent blacks away empty-handed. In addition to the watermelons, barbecue, and whiskey for participating voters, there were the Negro jobs on the city payroll. Police and fire department positions, to be sure, were reserved for whites at that time, but garbage collection and jobs at segregated public schools were open. The prestigious jobs at the federal post office were also handled by black members of the Crump machine when Republicans were in the White House. During the twenties, all but 36 of the 159 city mail carriers were black.

Republican politics offered Memphis blacks an opportunity to gain recognition and status. Since there were so few white Republi-

24. *Ibid.,* 18–9; Walter P. Adkins, "Beale Street Goes to the Polls" (M.A. thesis, Ohio State Univ., 1935), 22–25.
25. *Commercial Appeal,* Oct. 14, 1917.
26. Kenneth D. Wald, "Machine Politics in Memphis: The Case of the Missing Ethnics" (unpublished paper by a political scientist at Memphis State University).

cans in Memphis, blacks could easily dominate the party, and Robert R. Church, Jr. was thus able to be the most prominent Republican leader. Church had grown up in a brown mansion with crystal chandeliers and mahogany mantels, attended Oberlin College, and reluctantly entered his father's Solvent Savings Bank as a cashier in 1907. But when the father died in 1912, the twenty-seven-year-old son felt free to withdraw from the bank and devote himself to the game of politics. Church enlisted the assistance of the black middle class and created the Lincoln League to urge black voters to register and pay their poll taxes. More than ten thousand blacks were registered, one-third of the city's total in 1916. Church then ran black candidates for Congress and the state legislature. The black candidates did not expect to win, but they did gain national Republican recognition for Church. He became the most influential local politician in the party and the leading black adviser to the Republican national chairman. During the twenties he controlled the Republican patronage for Memphis. His decision appointed the local post office personnel. Of course, he had to obey local custom and appoint white men to the executive positions. The federal marshals, prosecuting attorneys, and judges also had to be white, but it was a measure of black power to confer with Boss Crump on the candidates and to make the selection from among white applicants.[27]

As long as Republicans ruled the White House, Robert Church worked as a useful part of the Crump machine, using his influence for the Democratic Crump ticket in local and state elections, then protecting the machine from any federal prosecution by appointing sympathetic Republican federal officials—especially the local attorney general—and by passing the word to Mr. Crump if a Republican senator planned an investigation of election fraud in Shelby County. After the Democrats ended Republican patronage with the election of Franklin D. Roosevelt, however, Boss Crump could control the patronage through his own party and no longer needed his aristocratic black Republican. Church was very vulnerable because

27. Tucker, *Lieutenant Lee of Beale Street,* 68–90; Paul Lewinson, *Race, Class, & Party: A History of Negro Suffrage and White Politics in the South* (New York: Grosset, 1959), 138–41; Annette E. Church, *The Robert R. Churches of Memphis* (Ann Arbor: Edwards Bros., 1974).

he had paid no city taxes on his real estate properties; so Crump simply had the property confiscated by local government and sold for back taxes, impoverishing Church and driving him from the city.[28]

The elimination of Robert Church from the machine in 1939 appeared to mark a general repression of black freedom. An International Longshoremen's organizer was almost killed by the city police after he attempted to recruit black workers at the Wolf River Transportation Company. J.B. Martin, a druggist who had once been an important part of the machine, was threatened with jail and forced out of town after he openly criticized bossism. Other middle-class critics were intimidated by Crump's police commissioner, Joe Boyle, who warned:

> We have our eyes on five Negro preachers, four Negro doctors, one Negro barbecue and restaurant operator, two Negro postmen, five Negro newspaper writers, one Negro drugstore operator, one Negro undertaker, who have been fanning race hatred.
>
> Should anything happen in Memphis these nineteen will be largely responsible for it.
>
> I say again this is a white man's country, and always will be and any Negro who doesn't agree to this had better move on.
>
> After we have dealt with the small discordant element, which is no advantage to their race or its relation with the white people, we then hope we can go along on fair and peaceful terms with the many very excellent, well meaning Negro preachers, doctors, lawyers, teachers, postal employees, and other Negroes.[29]

Boss Crump himself phoned the black editor of Memphis *World* and warned:

> You have a bunch of niggers teaching social equality, stirring up social hatred. I am not going to stand for it. I've dealt with niggers all my life and I know how to treat them. That darn paper is using Communistic propaganda—we are not going to put up with Pittsburgh stuff here. This is Memphis.
>
> We will deal with them in no uncertain terms and it won't be in the dark—it will be broad daylight. You be sure to tell them I said so. We

28. Ralph J. Bunche, *The Political Status of the Negro in the Age of F.D.R.* ed. Dewey W. Grantham (Chicago: Univ. of Chicago Press, 1973), 493–502.

29. *Memphis Press-Scimitar,* Dec. 11, 1940; Utillus R. Phillips to Frank Murphy, May 27, 1939, Box C-367, NAACP Papers (Washington: Manuscripts Division, Library of Congress); Tucker, *Lieutenant Lee of Beale Street,* 127–29.

are not going to tolerate a bunch of niggers spreading racial hatred and running things their way. Tell them Mr. Crump said so. You understand me?[30]

Crump intimidated his critics and continued to rule this major city with a black population of more than one hundred thousand people who were restricted to second-class citizenship inferior to that enjoyed by blacks in Northern cities such as Chicago, Cleveland, Pittsburgh, or New York. While no black Memphians had been elected to office since the nineteenth century, blacks in Chicago and Cleveland obtained growing political influence in the twentieth century after first electing representatives to their city councils in 1915. In New York the first black alderman won in 1919, and by 1944 Adam Clayton Powell, Jr. would go to Congress. Black Memphis voted but lagged further and further behind in political status.

Boss Crump did continue to offer paternalism—welfare, health care, public housing, schools, playgrounds, and personal favors. If a black pastor were about to lose his favorite choir director because of the economic advantages in Los Angeles or Detroit, a visit to a black machine leader—Lieutenant George W. Lee or Reverend Blair T. Hunt—could secure a Crump-approved city job or post office position to hold the choir director in Memphis. Crump also sought to control racial violence, seeking to protect blacks from white aggression. He had always opposed the Klan (which was bitterly anti-machine), and he promised to prevent any pogrom such as the 1919 Chicago riot, which killed twenty-three blacks, the East St. Louis riot, with its death toll of thirty-nine, or the 1943 Detroit riot, with twenty-five black deaths. The machine provided security for blacks and also delivered a better share of city services and less brutal police treatment than did white rule in those Southern cities where blacks did not vote.[31] So blacks followed the machine loyally and voted as they were instructed.

30. James C. Dickerson statement, Oct. 30, 1940, Edward Meeman Papers, Mississippi Valley Collection; interview with James H. Purdy, Oct. 20, 1973; Saunders Redding, *No Day of Triumph* (New York: Harper, 1942), 175–83.

31. Gunnar Myrdal, *An American Dilemma: The Negro Problem and Modern Democracy* (New York: Harper, 1944), 499; for the Klan in Memphis, see Kenneth T. Jackson, *The Ku Klux Klan in the City 1915–1930* (New York: Oxford Univ. Press, 1967), 53.

Memphis may have been like a Southern town in denying blacks the status of political office-holding and in segregating its public facilities, yet city government functioned in much the same manner as in any Northern machine. The Boss sought to win votes by controlling ethnic conflicts and delivering city services and personal favors. Blacks shared access in a system not unlike that of most metropolitan governments. The machine in Dixie was as pragmatic as any Northern organization. To silence black protest, the machine might claim that Memphis was a "white man's country," but on other occasions the organization would quote Abraham Lincoln to the black community, promising that the city government would do for "a community of people whatever they need to have done but cannot do at all or cannot do so well for themselves in their separate and individual capacities."[32]

Few pockets of resistance to the political machine surfaced in the Memphis ghettoes. Certainly no organized resistance emerged until 1948, when the wealthiest capitalist in black Memphis, Dr. J.E. Walker, opposed Crump's choice for U.S. senator. A business entrepreneur, Walker had become a leader with prestige in his community as his insurance company, Universal Life, expanded to eight states and gained more than two million dollars of assets. The Mississippi-born émigré with an M.D. from Meharry Medical School had made his insurance company a success and then assumed a leadership role in the local chapter of the National Association for the Advancement of Colored People and the Urban League. On the national level, Walker served as president of the National Negro Business League during the forties. He was, to be sure, a cautious man, but if the revolt against the machine seemed likely to succeed, he and the director of the Urban League, Reverend J.A. McDaniel, would join the Congress of Industrial Organizations and the civic reformers in a rebellion against Boss Crump.[33]

32. *Benefits and Opportunities for Colored Citizens of Memphis 1940–1944* (Memphis: City of Memphis, 1945).
33. Tucker, *Lieutenant Lee of Beale Street,* 121–2, 146; interview with J.A. McDaniel, Dec. 14, 1966; interview with Taylor C.D. Hayes, Nov. 30, 1966.

2.

Mister Crump

In more than a hundred years of existence, Memphis had produced no statesman whom her citizens cared to dignify with a bronze statue. The history of the lusty river town had little to do with statesmanship, learning, or intellect. The story described murder, hardwood lumbering, and the cotton capital of the world; it also encompassed the tragedy of a deadly plague of tropical yellow fever. The heroes of the unhealthy and immoral river town had not been gentlemen politicians. They had been rough and ambitious upstart businessmen such as Nathan Bedford Forrest, the slave trader and Confederate cavalry leader whose maxim had been "Git thar fustest with the mostest." Napoleon Hill, the crafty speculator, avoided military service in the Civil War and then, as a cotton merchant with "bull luck," became the town's first millionaire even though he continued to spit on the floor. The economic elite of Memphis, the cotton brokers and factors on Front Street, gave little attention to local government. They had largely abandoned it to the Irish immigrants since the 1850s. Honorable reputations had not been earned in local politics during the nineteenth century. By the end of the century, however, as the Memphis population increased to more than one hundred thousand, past civic neglect was an embarrassment to the growing number of respectable citizens who longed for their town to become a decent place, a city of good repute.[1] Any politician who successfully claimed credit for cleaning up the river town would surely be awarded not only a statue but also sainthood in his own time.

Control of local government had fallen to more than five hundred Memphis saloonkeepers. The largely Irish and Italian bartenders ran both neighborhood establishments and scandalous dives with reputations for robbing country boys outright and by means of booze, gambling, and sex. The keepers of dives protected themselves from the law by political organization; they paid poll taxes for other voters and produced the tax receipts on election day to win majorities for friendly candidates and thus insure that their interests would be protected from law enforcement. Memphis saloonkeepers maintained only a loosely organized machine not yet dominated by a single boss, but their city governments were considered expensive and inefficient as well as immoral by the new middle class of Memphis. In 1903 Walker Wellford, a local barrel manufacturer who wanted paved streets for Memphis, demanded that the mayor open the city books so that voters could see why the city had too little money to begin street paving.[2]

Wellford and his reform group of businessmen and clergy organized and won a share of local government in 1905, electing James Malone as their mayor. The city books were now annually audited, and street paving began. But the saloonkeepers still owned councilmen and the vice-mayor, and tension between the two groups created bickering, inefficiency, and an opportunity for a new politician to rise to power by building an organization with support from both reformers and saloonkeepers.

The young Memphis boss, E. H. Crump, was a fiercely competitive redhead with the soul and discipline of a business tycoon. He was a small-town Mississippi youth who had come up to Memphis as a bookkeeper in the 1890s, married the daughter of a wealthy

---

1. See Gerald Capers, *The Biography of a River Town: Memphis, Its Heroic Age* (Chapel Hill: Univ. of North Carolina Press, 1939); Shields McIlwaine, *Memphis Down in Dixie* (New York: Dutton, 1948); and William D. Miller, *Memphis During the Progressive Era* (Memphis: Memphis State Univ. Press, 1957).

2. Miller, *Memphis During the Progressive Era,* 87–89, 127–47.

merchant, and used the old man's credit to buy himself a business. He then took up politics, winning elections as councilman and then as the mayor who inaugurated a new commission form of government in 1909, all without making a single political speech. Devoid of oratorical ability himself, he did have the genius of understanding human nature and organizing others who could make speeches and negotiate with the ward bosses. Crump recognized in Frank J. Rice, a Memphis-born Irish-Italian, the political acumen and expertise on which to build a winning organization. The Memphis Irish-Italian and the Mississippi Anglo-Saxon joined together, one managing the back rooms of the organization and the other the front office, an unbeatable combination. While Mayor Crump made a show of being the efficient progressive who would suppress vice and inaugurate good government, the underworld of open gambling, prostitution, and illegal alcohol continued to contribute protection money. Police Chief William J. Hayes later testified in court that as much as $80,000 was collected in a single year. Crump may have been honest in not using the tainted money for his private purposes, but his organization was certainly corrupt in purchasing sufficient poll taxes to control elections. C.P.J. Mooney, editor of the local *Commercial Appeal,* and Tennessee Governor Ben W. Hooper led the opposition to these illegal practices and forced Crump from office in 1915 by court action charging him with failure to enforce the state prohibition law. While loss of office was embarrassing, Ed Crump never admitted guilt. He insisted instead that he had been victimized by evil private power corporations which had so feared his plan for municipally owned electricity that they had become the secret force behind his ouster. Crump's public relations campaign would later succeed so fully that his story was accepted as true even though no evidence supported it.[3]

3. William D. Miller initially doubted Crump's alibi (Miller, *Memphis During the Progressive Era,* 225, n71). Still, in his next book—*Mr. Crump of Memphis* (Baton Rouge: Louisiana State Univ. Press, 1964), 114–16—he seemed to accept the account Crump told 33 years after the event. For the response of a corporation attorney (Lovick P. Miles), see the *Memphis Press-Scimitar,* Aug. 29, 1949; see also Allen H. Kitchens, "Ouster of Mayor Edward H. Crump 1915–1916," *West Tennessee Historical Society Papers* 19 (1965), 105–20; Lamar Whitlow Bridges, "Editor Mooney Versus Boss Crump," *West Tennessee Historical Society Papers* 20 (1966),

Uncritical acceptance of his explanation later created the impression that Crump had indeed been a sincere progressive like Samuel "Golden Rule" Jones of Toledo or Tom Johnson of Cleveland. Crump, it is true, did make occasional rhetorical attacks on the utility corporations owned by Wall Street, but in his years as mayor he never extended municipal ownership to a single utility; he never secured a lower streetcar fare or a cheaper electric rate. His anti-corporation achievements were modest—he pressured the streetcar company into adding a crosstown line, and he persuaded the railroads to build eleven street underpasses. Crump surely could have won more from the utilities, but his main concern had never been social reform; his interest lay in city administration. He had gained power as the businessman's candidate who asserted: "Memphis should be conducted as a great business corporation." He did run an efficient government, winning more effort from the health, fire, and police departments. He claimed that the increased efficiency allowed a lower tax rate, and he did reduce the tax rate, but he more than compensated for the rate reduction by raising property assessments 30 percent. Mayor Crump surely demonstrated his mastery of advertising and public relations as well as administration.[4]

Crump's executive ability was also demonstrated by his creation of a successful political machine. On taking office he conducted a brief publicity war on vice but then permitted the underworld to run wide open. He and his associates could apparently negotiate successful understandings with the various contending groups in Memphis and also secure corrupt financing of the machine by an illegal underworld. Saloon and ballot corruption never led the voters to throw Crump out of office, however, just as San Franciscans never voted the corrupt Abe Ruef from office. Moralistic local progressives were unsuccessful until they turned to the courts to oust the machine. Crump's rise to the position of all-powerful urban boss

---

77–107; for court testimony of machine corruption, see Memphis *Commercial Appeal,* Oct. 14–15, 1917.

4. William Miller stresses Crump's rhetoric against utilities rather than questioning the meagerness of achievement, *Mr. Crump of Memphis,* 89–95; the only socialized utility, the water works, had been acquired in 1903 by the former machine mayor, John J. Williams.

was then temporarily checked, and his reputation as a progressive became somewhat tarnished.

Crump retreated to Shelby County politics and to his insurance business, keeping a low profile in city politics for a decade after his ouster, while the local business and civic leaders organized a Citizens League to secure good government, city planning, and a competent public health department.[5] In 1927, after Memphians tired of their competent reform mayor, Rowlett Paine, Crump again entered municipal politics. This time he pushed his own personal slate of candidates, headed by young Watkins Overton for mayor. A wealthy great-grandson of one of the land speculators who founded Memphis, Overton had studied at Harvard and the University of Chicago, been elected to the Tennessee state legislature, and had demonstrated the enthusiasm and sincerity that would appeal to those who had supported the reform mayor Paine. With attractive candidates such as Watkins Overton, the Crump ticket won part of the respectable vote and all the ward heeler ballots. With Crump men in all offices, the generation of absolute Crump control over local elections began.

When the newly elected Mayor Overton went to the insurance office of E. H. Crump and Company for instructions, Crump took out his scratch pad and wrote "good housekeeping." Watkins Overton relayed the charge to his fellow city commissioners, who took their notebooks and surveyed streets, alleys, and public buildings, noting faded paint, cracked windows, and broken streets, curbs, and sidewalks. Mr. Crump thought a cleanup good politics, and he toured the city streets weekly with his chauffeur and his secretary. He noted every minor public blemish and sent reports of the flaws to his mayor for immediate action. Crump dreamed of a beautiful city with swaying Paul Scarlet roses bordering the streets, majestic trees, neatly clipped lawns, and a citizenry grateful to their political leader. To enact his personal vision, he involved women of the com-

5. Virginia M. Phillips, "Rowlett Paine's First Term as Mayor of Memphis 1920–1924" (M.A. thesis, Memphis State Univ., 1958); Crump's activity during these years is reflected in his correspondence with Senator Kenneth D. McKellar, which is boxed separately in the McKellar Collection, Memphis-Shelby County Public Library.

munity by creating the City Beautiful Commission in 1930 and drafting prominent housewives to see his city beautified and kept as neat as a home. In each of the city's fifty-two political wards an appointed chairwoman would police the district, promoting paint, flowers, shrubs, garden clubs, and E. H. Crump. The City Beautiful Commission headquarters soon had a file index with a card for every building in Memphis, on which annual inspection reports were noted by women who were paid field secretaries. Citizens could not even safely ignore their back lawns and alleys for fear that City Beautiful alley parades with an automobile caravan of women and city officials might detect their clutter and hold their negligence up to public ridicule. The year-round surveillance may have been hard on the nonconformists, but the majority of Memphians were proud to help their city win annually the "Cleanest Town in Tennessee" award.[6]

More important than beautification, the Memphis cleanup continued the earlier sanitation campaign that had eliminated yellow fever at the beginning of the century. The number one health enemy was now regarded as malaria—the curse of chills and fever—which had always plagued the Mississippi Delta and made Memphis an unattractive location for industry. As many as a dozen persons per 100,000 still died annually from malaria in the early thirties. But the city sanitation engineer, Albert H. Fletcher, slowly gained control over the malaria mosquitoes, filling in bayous, lining ditches with concrete, requiring screens for windows, and spraying oil on the breeding waters. As the campaign against chills and fever began to be won, Memphis obtained a large Firestone Tire and Rubber plant, which opened in 1937 and began to add industrial balance to the city's cotton, lumber, and merchandising.[7]

The energetic and efficient Crump government not only attracted

6. Frances Akers Greeson, *Memphis: The City Beautiful* (Memphis: City Beautiful Commission, 1947); Watkins Overton, "Statement Given to the *Commercial Appeal* Dec. 11, 1947," Box 13, Watkins Overton Papers, Mississippi Valley Collection; Memphians erroneously believe that their award was given to the city found "cleanest in America," a mistake no doubt resulting from Crump's public relations.

7. Watkins Overton, "Albert H. Fletcher: A Story of Achievement," Box 4, Overton Papers; Memphis and Shelby County Health Department, *Protecting Your Health* (Memphis: Health Department, 1945), 31–32.

industry and won city awards, but also bought out the privately owned electric and gas company and still managed to lower taxes. The property tax rate had been $2.25 but Crump began annual reductions of a few pennies a year in the early thirties and again lowered the rate in the forties until it finally stood at $1.80, much lower than in comparable cities such as Nashville, where the rate was $2.30, and Dallas, where it was $2.85. Memphians received such efficient and inexpensive government from such a personable, paternalistic boss that Mr. Crump need not have used illegal voting to retain power in Memphis. But he was never content with control of only city and county government; he wished to dominate the whole state of Tennessee. To be sure, an unfriendly rural legislature and governor could pass legislation very damaging to a local political machine. If Crump were to be secure in his control of Memphis, he needed friendly governors. And why should he not elect his own U.S. senators from Tennessee as well as his governors? State control required all the illegal votes his organization could manufacture, and any newspaper reporter who happened to capture fraudulent election practices on film was certain to be beaten with Mr. Crump's approval. Consider the case of Turner Catledge, the *Commercial Appeal* reporter who later became managing editor of the *New York Times.* While Catledge photographed and interviewed poor blacks whose votes were being cast repeatedly and fraudulently, the Shelby County assistant attorney general, Will Gerber, drove up and cursed Catledge, slapped him around, destroyed the photographs, and let his machine henchmen administer a beating. The angry and bleeding reporter then rushed to Crump, seeking justice.

> "Boy, tell me who did this to you," Mr. Crump said. "Nobody can do this to a friend of mine and get away with it."
> "Willie Gerber did it to me," Catledge explained.
> "We've got to do something about this. . . . What do you suggest?
> "Fire the son of a bitch!"
> Crump looked thoughtful. "Oh no, boy, that's not enough. We've got to do something more than that. . . . I'll tell you what we're going to do, Catledge. From now on, you stay away from places like that or else some day you may really get hurt."[8]

8. Turner Catledge, *My Life and The Times* (New York: Harper, 1971), 43–7;

Fraudulent expansion of the Shelby County vote and intimidation of newspaper reporters who sought to document it permitted Crump to control state elections. The two-dollar poll tax had kept so many of the two and a half million Tennesseans from casting ballots at the beginning of the Great Depression that the state Democratic primary could be won by little more than 100,000 votes, and in Shelby County alone the Crump organization could produce one-third of those needed. In the 1932 state Democratic primary the Crump organization did manufacture the necessary vote and smashed the cameras of reporters who sought the evidence of vote fraud. With the election of Governor Hill McAlister, Crump's absolute control of state politics began. Four years later the major opposition paper conceded defeat when Crump merely announced his candidate for governor. "Tennessee's gubernatorial primary was settled late Saturday," the Nashville *Tennessean* said. "Boss Edward Hull Crump of Memphis spectacularly wrote 'finis' to a gubernatorial campaign that had raged for a month. With Shelby enlisted for Browning, there is no actual race."[9]

Crump's man, Gordon Browning, did win the 1936 gubernatorial election with 60,218 votes from Shelby County, while the major opponent was permitted only 861. But Governor Browning then had the audacity to think he was independent of Boss Crump. "You can ride on my wagon all you want but you can't drive. That's my job," Browning told the furious old boss. Thus began a monumental power struggle as the governor sent spies and undercover agents into Memphis and the Crump organization countered with counterspies and occasional beatings of Browning men. This time the organization apparently feared to stuff the ballot boxes in black precincts and instead put pressure on the white wards. A larger white turnout, which almost offset the decline in fraudulent voting in black wards,

---

Crumpites believe that a little brutality and voting fraud were necessary because without the election of friendly governors, Crump would never be safe in his control of Memphis. It is still said that Crump was never "power-hungry" but only "interested in Memphis."

9. Jennings Perry, *Democracy Begins at Home: The Tennessee Fight for the Poll Tax* (Philadelphia: Lippincott, 1944), 10; V. O. Key, Jr., *Southern Politics in State and Nation* (New York: Knopf, 1949), 59–61; *Commercial Appeal,* Aug. 5, 1932.

produced 56,000 votes against the governor and only 9,000 for him.[10]

With the 1938 election Crump apparently learned he could win without the worst of his organization's old voting practices. He no longer needed to tolerate the vice that had made him the subject of much criticism. He had earlier ended the numbers lottery or policy racket, throwing about two thousand policy writers out of work after *Collier's* and *Time's* disclosures of sin in Memphis had embarrassed him. Now that Prohibition was being repealed in Tennessee, making bars and booze legal, only prostitution and gambling remained to make political payoffs. Crump's oldest and closest lieutenants—Frank Rice and W. Tyler McLain—died in 1938, and perhaps he was left without anyone he could trust with the sensitive liaison between vice and politics. The federal Department of Justice, which had cleaned up New Orleans, threatened to send a special prosecutor to Memphis. So in 1940 Mr. Crump appointed a new police commissioner—Joe Boyle—to shut down the whorehouses and end organized vice in Memphis. Poll taxes were no longer purchased with vice money, but the contributions of the city employees and Memphis businessmen built a respectable campaign fund sufficient to assist those who, according to Crump, "could not pay their own poll taxes. . . ."[11]

Without the restraint of Frank Rice and W. Tyler McLain, men who called Ed Crump by his first name and told him when he was wrong, the Boss could play a game of musical chairs with his political offices. He capriciously banished City Commissioner Clifford Davis to Washington, D.C., where he replaced Congressman Walter Chandler, who in turn replaced Mayor Watkins Overton. The dapper Watkins had remained an efficient mayor, but he had failed to remain completely subservient. Even though Overton had consulted faithfully with Mr. Crump while negotiating the city pur-

10. Joseph H. Riggs (ed.), *Gordon Browning: An Oral Memoir* (Memphis: Memphis Public Library, 1966), 85–86; George R. King, "Browning Campaign—Police Reports," Box 1, Overton Papers; *Commercial Appeal,* Aug. 4, 1938.
11. Clark Porteous, "Memphis Politics—Past and Present," *The Egyptians* (1963) 45–67; Miller, *Mr. Crump of Memphis,* 221; Tucker, *Lieutenant Lee of Beale Street* (Nashville: Vanderbilt Univ. Press, 1971), 124–37.

30

chase of Memphis Power and Light, he unwisely permitted leading businessmen to praise him for the purchase agreement. Mr. Crump felt snubbed and angrily passed the word that Overton had bungled the utility negotiations, that he had failed to negotiate for the gas works as well, and that he had grown "too arrogant . . . too big for the job." With Crump's obvious encouragement, city officials began a flood of criticism against Overton, with the most petty jibes coming from Crump himself. It seems that the old man's indignation had been aroused when he learned that Mrs. Overton had remarked to friends at a Southwestern football game, "Mr. Crump has fine hats but nothing underneath them."[12]

The proud Watkins Overton refused to knuckle under, ask forgiveness, or accept Mr. Crump's greater wisdom. For more than a decade he had given Memphis good government that he believed had enhanced Crump's reputation and power. But now Overton was being made just another "hand-biting ingrate" and held up to public ridicule. With the support of only one of the four city commissioners, Ralph Picard, his former administrative assistant, Overton stood up and fought back. He labeled Crump a dictator and called for a municipal Hatch Act to break the machine by taking city employees out of politics. "I will never bow my knee to any tyrant," Overton declared. "I will never raise my hand in Nazi salute to any dictator."[13] He even hoped he might defeat the machine and entered his one loyal commissioner in the special congressional election. His candidate received fewer than fifteen hundred votes.

Mr. Crump was politically invincible. Most Memphians agreed that he had given them good government and low taxes. Thousands felt indebted to him for personal favors during the past thirty years —employment by the city, work for the Works Progress Administration, or charity during the depression years. He seemed to know the whole city population by name, each man and all his family. Decades of practicing the basic political art of making individuals

12. Overton, shorthand note, Oct. 26, 1938, Box 3, Overton Papers; *Commercial Appeal,* Nov. 27, 1938; Mrs. Sidney B. Daniel, supervisor of stenographic services at Memphis State University, deciphered the note.
13. *Commercial Appeal,* Dec. 19, 1939; Overton, "1940 Statements," Box 4, Overton Papers.

feel important had made Mr. Crump an all-time champion. He was a most cordial man, tall and straight, with a mop of curly white hair crowned by specially built hats wider and taller than those of other people. He carried a walking cane and dressed in clothes that were natty and colorful. Mr. Crump had also mastered the public relations art of securing much public acclaim for charities that actually cost him very little. Every fall he organized his Mississippi riverboat ride for all the local shut-ins and orphans, and a football game at Crump Stadium with the proceeds going to the blind. There was also an E. H. Crump Day at the fairgrounds with free amusement rides, free lemonade, free cigars, free music, and free lapel streamers that said "Thank You Mister Crump." If Crump wanted to substitute a new mayor, certainly the people thought he knew what was best for them.

The unbroken series of election victories for Crump's candidates demoralized the opposition and created a widespread defeatist attitude that opposition votes were never counted and that Crump's election officials were sure to identify and turn in the name of every opposition voter. Control over the city was so tight and absolute that for two decades city elections were uncontested; only Crump's slate announced candidacy for office, while others were persuaded that they were "crazy" even to consider running against the political machine. The organization not only held control of the election machinery in every ward and precinct; it had also taken over every civic, religious, cultural, fraternal, and occupational organization. Crump lawyers on the public payroll had gained control of the local bar association. Crump men dominated the Knights of Columbus and B'nai B'rith as well as the Parent Teachers Association and the American Federation of Labor locals. By the thirties Crump could delight in comparing himself with Phillip II of Spain who, when urged by his confessors to forgive his enemies, had said, "Bless your heart, I have none. I have killed them all." Opposition simply wilted before Crump's power, although his organization never actually killed anyone. A widespread voluntary espionage system conveyed critical remarks directly to Mr. Crump, and the old man promoted fear of his system by exaggerating the effectiveness of his grapevine, suggesting that even a mildly critical remark would be reported to him "within five minutes." Physical violence for critics was also a "regrettable" probability. "We have friends everywhere," Crump admitted. "The man who talks against the administration is liable to get into trouble. Human nature being what it is, it is possible to get in a fight at any time at the polls with my sympathizers."[14]

The Crump organization easily intimidated those newcomers who moved into Memphis. After a Michigan businessman constructed a new jewelry store on Main Street, the city building inspector informed him that the front of his building violated the city code and would have to be rebuilt. The alarmed jeweler called his contractor, who assured him that the problem was political rather than structural. "Do you have any insurance from Mr. Crump?" the builder asked. "I suggest you take at least part of your insurance from E. H. Crump and Company." The jeweler purchased a policy from Crump, and the city inspector promptly approved the new store. Thus the merchant learned the political and economic realities of doing business in Memphis; in fact, forty years later he still preferred, for business reasons, that he not be personally identified as either a critic or a victim of Crump.

Mr. Crump would not tolerate criticism and a single call to an employer would quickly clarify for the troublemaker that "no young man can succeed in Memphis unless he is friendly to the Crump organization." Most Memphis businessmen could not afford to permit their employees to exercise freedom of speech. Consider the example of Walter Wallace, an indignant young chemist who so resented Mr. Crump's plan to extend local censorship from movies to books that he addressed a letter of protest to the *Memphis Press-Scimitar*:

> This censorship of books and literature is enough to make the blood boil in any American who has been taught that dictatorship and censorship are synonymous. It is sickening enough for our rights as movie fans to be throttled.
>
> The most nauseating part of the whole affair is that our so-called benevolent first citizen, Mr. Crump, is the originator of the plan. . . .

14. Spencer R. McCulloch, "Ed Crump the Big Boss of Memphis," St. Louis *Post-Dispatch,* July 3, 1938; *Chicago Tribune,* April 2, 9, 1939; E. H. Crump to Kenneth McKellar, Jan. 20, 1936, Box 2, Overton Papers.

> This censorship of books and literature is only a stepping stone to
> more and more censorship. What will the next idea be that will force us
> to bow to the wishes of the Crump machine?[15]

The very afternoon that the letter appeared in print, Wallace was
called in and fired by his employer, Clyde Collins, Incorporated. He
had attacked the political organization, which purchased 20,000
gallons of artificial lemonade from Clyde Collins for the E.H.
Crump Day at the fairgrounds. Not only was Wallace fired, he was
also insulted in a public letter that Mr. Crump sent to the *Press-
Scimitar.* A letter from Crump usually let the public know that the
critic was a public enemy, "a mangy bubonic rat," "an insipid ass,"
or a "low filthy scoundrel, pervert, degenerate."[16]

Fear of Crump's personal invective had been one of the strongest
deterrents against criticism. The old man had gleefully mastered the
art of writing personal attacks until only the brave or foolish were
willing to expose themselves to the vituperative ridicule which Crump
regularly used against critics, political opponents, and especially
Edward J. Meeman, the editor of the *Memphis Press-Scimitar.*

The bachelor editor had always been a crusader. Born in 1889,
the intellectual son of German-American parents in Evansville, Indiana, Meeman reacted to the widespread poverty he saw as a young
reporter by becoming a socialist. After a decade of party membership, he began moving politically to the right and ended an individ-
ualist who gave copies of Ralph Waldo Emerson's *Essays* to his
friends and opposed every concentration of power. Meeman believed, much like the Nashville Agrarians, that all men should own
property and thus be free and independent of employer, union, or
government. He encouraged federal efforts such as the Tennessee
Valley Authority and the Resettlement Administration, which encouraged people to live in rural America. But he so feared the New
Deal centralization of power that in 1940 he opposed President
Franklin D. Roosevelt's reelection and thereafter consistently supported Republicans for the presidency. As one who favored the
greatest freedom for the individual and resisted dangerous accumu-

15. *Memphis Press-Scimitar,* Nov. 8, 1946.
16. E. H. Crump to *Press-Scimitar,* Nov. 8, 1946; "Walter Wallace manuscript,"
Nov. 11, 1946, Edward J. Meeman Papers, Mississippi Valley Collection.

lations of power, Meeman began criticizing the Crump organization soon after assuming the *Press-Scimitar* editorship in 1931.[17]

Meeman had been a brilliant success in the newspaper business before moving to Memphis. The Scripps-Howard chain had transferred him south from Indiana in 1921 to begin a paper in Knoxville, Tennessee. The *News* grew to be the number one Knoxville daily and made its editor a member of the local power structure, respected for his financial success and his editorial campaigns for public power, council-manager government, and the Great Smoky Mountains National Park. In moving on to Scripps-Howard's *Memphis Press-Scimitar* in 1931, Meeman accepted the challenge to see if he could again lead a newspaper to success. But in Memphis he encountered the hostility of the Crump machine, which had no use for crusading editors. As Mayor Watkins Overton told Mr. Crump in 1933, "I agree with you, we will never be able to tie to him. . . . Meeman thinks the 'machine' is about gone and is trying to educate the people so there will be what he calls 'good government' to take its place. Meeman says he likes a lot of things you do and a lot of things the city does, but he does not approve of our election methods and thinks we make people afraid of us by using our power."[18]

Meeman at first believed the Crump organization to be just another political machine, but he later observed that Crump had become a dictator. Memphians had so abdicated their responsibilities that they left all problems to the wisdom of the leader who operated a spy system and terrorized or demoralized all opposition. "I was to have," Meeman later said, "the rare experience of operating a free press under a totalitarian dictatorship which controlled nearly everything in town—not only politics and government, but the Bar Association, the Parent Teacher Association, the Council of Civic Clubs, the American Legion, the labor unions, the business community."[19]

Meeman never stood quite alone. He had firm support from his employer, the Scripps-Howard newspaper chain, which purchased

17. Edward J. Meeman, "Autobiography," unpublished book manuscript, Meeman Papers.
18. Watkins Overton to E. H. Crump, April 17, 1933, Box 2, Overton Papers.
19. Meeman, "Autobiography"; Meeman to John Temple Graves, Sept. 29, 1946, Meeman Papers.

the *Commercial Appeal* in 1936 and thereby owned both local dailies, one that opposed Mr. Crump and one that did not. In addition to protection and encouragement from his employer, Meeman also had the support of his religion. An unorthodox Christian whose views about the Bible were those of a Unitarian, Meeman nevertheless was a passionate mystic. His emotional fervor had been awakened in 1936 by the Moral Re-Armament movement, which taught acceptance of the four ethical absolutes—absolute honesty, absolute purity, absolute unselfishness, and absolute love—and advocated the techniques of observing a quiet time each day to secure guidance from God and joining a small intimate group to share religious experience. Meeman organized his own interdenominational circle in Memphis and took prayer seriously. He believed with the Christian Scientists that God would respond to requests for healings.[20]

Secure in his faith, his individualism, and his profession, Meeman battled the Crump dictatorship, warning his readers:

> Almost everyone in Memphis realizes that we are not dealing merely with "machine politics" in the old sense, but with the phenomenon of dictatorship. The question is whether the people will remain content with that. If the predominantly Anglo-Saxon population of Memphis remains content to give up democracy, what hope is there that the Anglo-Saxon world will remain free?[21]

If only ten leading citizens would band together and criticize the Crump government, Meeman insisted, they could easily convert it from a dictatorship to an agency of democracy. When Crump blundered into appointing a succession of weak mayors at the end of the Second World War, Meeman was certain that a citizens' revolt was near, that "the people are hungering for democracy in this city. This is the hour."[22]

The organization had long sought to discredit Meeman, but this time Crump insisted that Mayor James J. Pleasants read into the minutes of the Memphis City Commission an allegation that Mee-

20. Meeman, "Autobiography"; Meeman to Gertrude Meeman, June 29, 1965, Meeman Papers.
21. *Memphis Press-Scimitar,* Jan. 26, 1944.
22. *Ibid.,* May 12, 1947.

man was a homosexual or, as the mayor phrased it, "one of those things." Pleasants further said:

> Meeman has long and futilely attempted to have weight in the political thought of this community. He has failed in every election. He has been branded as a low, contemptible liar time and time again by any number of men who are highly respected.
>
> Only a man with a perverted and degenerate mind stoops to lie about anyone. It's the mark of a coward who feels he can lie through the columns of his newspaper with impunity.[23]

The slurs and allegations, for which Pleasants later attempted to apologize, were then printed as a pamphlet—"Liars Will Steal"—and mailed out to the public. Having been read into a city legislative proceeding, the slanderous remarks were exempt from libel suit and Meeman had no adequate protection. Certainly Memphians would never protest this brutal and irregular use of political power to discredit a critic. Fewer than half a dozen letters of complaint were sent to Mayor Pleasants.[24]

Memphians had been propagandized into believing that the *Memphis Press-Scimitar* was no more than a scandal sheet, while Mr. Crump was indeed the "Founder of Modern Memphis," responsible for every achievement in the past half-century, liberator of the oppressed river city from "entrenched corporations", and maker of a clean, beautiful, and highly moral city. During every political campaign the citizens were regularly subjected to indoctrination, even on the streetcars. The organization drafted young attorneys and sent them downtown to board the streetcars and deliver little two-minute orations between stops to the captive audiences. All city employees, including school teachers and librarians, were required to do election work, to praise Crump's wisdom and achievements. The city printed its own propaganda book, "Memphis: Civic Progress,"

23. Copies of *Liars Will Steal* are in Meeman Papers and also in 1947 Mayor's Correspondence, P file, Memphis City Archives, Memphis-Shelby County Public Library.

24. According to a *Press-Scimitar* reporter, "Pleasants never did get over doing this terrible thing he had not wanted to do. He used to ask me if there was some way he could make amends," Porteous, "Memphis Politics—Past and Present," 59; letters of complaint are found in 1947 Mayor's Correspondence, P file, Memphis City Archives.

which credited Crump with every civic reform since 1909. Thus, by the end of the Second World War, a generation of Memphians had been raised to believe that the old man was the greatest Memphian and that criticizing him was criticizing one's own city.[25]

Even Crump's biographer would fall into the habit of crediting every city project to the foresight of the boss. McKellar Lake, the industrial harbor on the Mississippi River, provided one case in point. For years the chamber of commerce had talked of the need for industrial sites on the river without ever receiving any support from Mr. Crump. Then a river engineer, General Max Tyler, suggested turning part of the Mississippi into a lake. Just below Memphis, where President's Island splits the Mississippi, the Tennessee side could be dammed to create a still water lake stretching seven miles along the island and the Tennessee shore. It could provide a superb river port and miles of industrial building sites. The chamber of commerce succeeded in getting Crump's approval in 1945 to secure the fifty million dollars of federal funds for the Army Corps of Engineers to dam the Mississippi. After completion, McKellar Lake would, of course, be considered "another Crump-conceived project."[26]

The overwhelming majority of Memphians were happy to let Mr. Crump select their officials and manage their city. "What Mr. Crump liked—that's what we liked," they would later say. "And what he thought was nice—that's what we thought was nice." They took pride in the regular interest of national magazines in their Mister Crump. How many other towns could see their leader on the cover of *Time* magazine or read that their community was "no Kansas City. There is no graft, no corruption; Crump has never taken a cent from the public treasury, nor will he permit anyone else to do so. Gambling is abolished, and crime has been cut down: Memphis is one of the few big cities with no policy or numbers racket, and prostitutes have been driven out."

It was true that outsiders had rather freely suggested that Crump,

25. John Gunther, *Inside U.S.A.* (New York: Harper, 1947), 749–54; Louise Gambill (ed.), *Memphis: Civic Progress* (Memphis: City of Memphis, 1945).

26. Miller, *Mr. Crump of Memphis,* 341; Memphis Chamber of Commerce, *Annual Report 1945,* 10–11; *Memphis Press-Scimitar,* Oct. 9, 1950; interview with Edmund Orgill, July 13, 1973.

like the fascist dictators of Europe, was an enemy of democracy. Jennings Perry, editor of the Nashville *Tennessean,* penned an angry denunciation, *Democracy Begins at Home* (Philadelphia, 1944), explaining how the "arrogant, vain, vindictive, self-righteous old man" had frustrated the state campaign to repeal the poll tax and free Tennessee from one-man rule. The *Washington Post* saw Memphis as a warning that even in America the people would bow down to a fascist dictatorship:

> Memphis, Tennessee, should be a warning to the whole country. The city is a perfect example of the ease with which Americans with a philosophy of efficiency and materialism can succumb to fascism and like it. The majority of the citizens of Memphis lick the boots of their notorious tyrant, Mr. E.H. Crump, not because they have to. They lick his boots because it pays.
>
> Like all fascist rulers, Crump has the support and admiration of big business. "We do not approve of his methods but we are enthusiastic about his results," was the way one businessman put it. "Our city is the most efficient in the whole U.S.A. We have a nationally famous health department and safety program, good schools, sanitation, recreation facilities and fire department. With all these advantages we have low insurance and tax rates. So why worry how it is done."[27]

These outside criticisms of Crump offended the vast majority of Memphians, who could never believe their leader was a fascist. He, like most of them, had been a country boy from Mississippi who came to Memphis to make good. He had built Memphis, they believed, into the South's most promising city and had given it control over the state of Tennessee. Only an outsider from the North, such as Edward J. Meeman, could misunderstand the leadership that Mr. Crump had given the Bluff City. Proud of Memphis and fiercely loyal to their leader, Memphians appeared unlikely to rebel against Mister Crump in 1948.[28]

27. *Washington Post,* May 13, 1946.
28. *Time* 47 (May 27, 1946); George Craig Leake, "A Presentation of the Script and Production Background for the Television Documentary 'The Once and Always Mister Crump,' " (M.A. thesis, Memphis State Univ., 1968).

3.

The Federal Unionists

The revolt against Mr. Crump emerged from a small cluster of liberals whose major concern was the union of America with the democratic nations of Western Europe. The group united around one book—Clarence Streit's *Union Now* (1940). Streit, an international reporter for the *New York Times,* had watched the League of Nations fail to stand against military aggressions of Japan, Italy, and Germany in the 1930s. He then argued that Western civilization was bound for destruction unless the democracies united under a new government that would take over common defense, currency, and trade just as the individual states of North America had once united and turned these common problems over to the United States federal government. He contended that wars would become more and more terrible and perhaps democracy would end completely unless federal union could be accepted. The democracies owned most of the natural resources and two-thirds of the world trade but seemed less efficient than totalitarian governments in waging war. The democracies were so divided by nationalism—narrow self-interest and jealousy—that they refused to work together in the League of Nations. The League idea had failed completely. If individual rights and freedoms were to be preserved, the democracies of the North

Atlantic must unite in a federal union for common defense and the preservation of traditional freedoms.[1]

The Memphis movement for world federation began with a young attorney, Lucius E. Burch, Jr., son of a patrician Southern family. With a father who was dean of Vanderbilt University Medical School and an intellectual mother, young Lucius grew up on the family plantation in the Nashville suburbs, nursed by an old mammy who had once been a slave. He was much influenced by a maternal grandfather whose personal bookplates bore the motto "ubi libertas ibi patri"—where there is liberty there is the fatherland. Lucius also heard the Southern Agrarians (Robert Penn Warren, a member of the literary group, lived for two years on the Burch farm) lamenting the loss of the Civil War and the triumph of Northern capitalism. He grew up a Southern conservative and a physical fitness enthusiast who hunted eagles for bounty in Alaska and three times fought his way to the heavyweight boxing championship at Vanderbilt. After law school Lucius joined his uncle's Memphis firm in 1935. He intended to make money from the practice of corporation law and had no thought of engaging in liberal crusades. A confident attorney who defended the rights and liberties of his clients, however, was certain to encounter the opposition of Boss Crump. By the fall of 1940 Burch had aroused Mr. Crump's anger when he prepared a legal brief reminding the organization that Mr. Crump had no constitutional right to order a gambler to "get out of town." Burch's legal dissent and arrogant independence caused the Crump organization to consider him a member of the opposition camp, and surely the experience of being ostracized and labeled a dissenter made Burch more sympathetic to liberal thought. Although a Southern sectionalist by birth and education, he became a man of intellect whose mind was not locked to traditional wisdom. He would read the new literature on race and reject the belief in black inferiority; he would also read Clarence Streit's *Union Now* and become an internationalist.[2]

1. Clarence K. Streit, *Union Now: The Proposal for Inter-Democracy Federal Union* (New York: Harper, 1940).
2. Lucius E. Burch, Jr. to Edward J. Meeman, Feb. 14, 1956, Meeman Papers, Missisippi Valley Collection; *Memphis Press-Scimitar,* April 19, 1961; *Commercial*

Burch gave a copy of *Union Now* to Edward J. Meeman, whom he admired for writing so freely and independently in Boss Crump's city. Although Burch and Meeman were very different personalities —Burch had no religion and his pleasures included hunting, fishing, smoking, and drinking, while the ascetic Meeman attended weekly prayer meetings and looked with horror on all sports involving bloodshed—they were both devoted to individual freedoms which the Crump organization so frequently violated. *Union Now,* with its emphasis on the preservation of individual freedom, became one of Meeman's causes, and the two men became close friends. Meeman gave Burch a copy of Ralph Waldo Emerson's *Essays* to applaud his individual courage. "I am not surprised that you find Emerson to your liking," Meeman later told Lucius, "because you are more like the people of his day than of ours."[3]

Through the Second World War Lucius Burch propagandized his narrow circle of friends by advocating federal union before a local intellectual society—The Egyptians—and distributing copies of *Union Now.* After the war he made his second major convert, Edmund Orgill.

Orgill was the head of a wholesale hardware firm that three English brothers had established in 1847. It was kept in the family and now covered the six-state Mid-South area with more than a hundred salesmen. In addition to being president of Orgill Brothers, he was a director of Union Planters National Bank, president of the Memphis Chamber of Commerce, and a generous fund raiser for worthy causes. Born in 1899, he was brought up to value plain living and family tradition. His father gently nurtured a sense of duty, checked the schoolboy's lessons every evening, and instilled a habit of diligence and obligation. Orgill earned a Phi Beta Kappa key at the University of Virginia and returned in 1920 to work in the family firm, wrapping packages at the parcel post counter. He worked his way up to the warehouse and then was sent out on the road in 1923

Appeal, Nov. 7, 1972; Lucius E. Burch, Jr., "Plan for Peace," *The Egyptians* (1942); *idem,* "Characteristics of the American Negro," *The Egyptians* (1948); *idem,* "Why I am a Liberal," *The Egyptians* (1975).

3. Meeman to Burch, Sept. 22, 1941; Meeman, "Autobiography," Meeman Papers.

to sell to Mississippi hardware stores. In 1926 Orgill married a Mississippi cotton planter's daughter, Catherine Dean, and returned to Memphis as a buyer for Orgill Brothers. Business was Orgill's passion; he had no hobbies. He went to work early and stayed late, avoiding civic affairs and all other distractions except the Episcopal church, which he devoutly attended. Only after his father died in 1940 and Orgill replaced him as president of the company did he enter civic affairs. As head of a major business in Memphis, he was pressured to participate, so he joined in the Boy Scout fund drive of 1941 and became chairman of the Community Fund drive of 1943, president of the Rotary Club, member of the Board of Regents of the University of the South, and president of the chamber of commerce in 1945.[4]

Although Orgill read little and was unfamiliar with *Union Now,* he thought seriously enough about world government to set down his ideas on paper:

> We should wage just as wholehearted a war for world wide peace as we did for military victory. . . . We know freedom of speech, freedom of religion, economic opportunity. . . . I think we should definitely state our aims and purposes and lead the way right now in the formation of world government, inviting those to join who hold the same beliefs and are willing to fight for them.[5]

Writing a position paper was unusual for the busy hardware man. A long business trip to New York by train in December 1945 provided the time to think about world government. During his college days in Virginia he had once been interested in foreign policy because President Woodrow Wilson advocated a League of Nations as a means of establishing permanent world peace. He had joined the army to help bring peace, but the First World War ended before Orgill completed his air force pilot training, and he was even more disappointed by the American failure to participate in the League. Twenty-five years later, another world war—and perhaps his reading of Edward Meeman's *Press-Scimitar*—troubled Orgill enough

4. Clark Porteous, *The First Orgill Century 1847–1947* (Memphis: Merrill Kremer, 1947); interview with Edmund Orgill, July 13, 1973.
5. "December 1945 statement," Edmund Orgill Papers, Mississippi Valley Collection.

about world peace that he dictated a personal statement to his wife Catherine who was traveling with him. He kept the statement until the following April, when Lucius Burch advocated federal union before the Rotary Club, and then Orgill sent the attorney a copy. Burch recognized a convert and sent over a copy of Clarence Streit's *Union Now* with the prediction that Orgill would think Streit was a great man because he thought as Orgill did.[6]

Edmund Orgill read Streit's book during the summer of 1946. He became such a believer that when Edward Meeman later asked him to participate in a local committee for the study of world government, he pressed for something more dramatic than a study group. "The thing to do is to bring Streit here," Orgill said. "Streit is right. We must protect our personal freedom." Orgill called Streit and persuaded him to come to Memphis. In the auditorium at local Southwestern College, the federal union advocate delivered an alarming speech—Communism had gobbled up central Europe, had moved into China, and was threatening Western Europe. Streit further elaborated on the world crisis at Meeman's rural estate, where he talked with Orgill, Burch, John Apperson, Gilmer Richardson, Winfield Qualls, Dr. Earle Scharff, and Edward Meeman. The discussion group decided that very evening to organize a Memphis chapter of Federal Union and to make Orgill president.

Edmund Orgill threw himself into the Federal Union movement with great zeal, delivering a speech a week before local civic clubs. He made no polished address, but his intense sincerity won converts. He explained that a union of the democracies could provide economic and military power that would prevent Russia from launching the third world war. The union of national armed forces would also permit enormous tax savings. The abolition of national trade barriers would create an Atlantic free trade area that would boom with economic activity and demonstrate to the rest of the world the effectiveness of real democracy. The new union would guarantee freedom, restore economic prosperity, and preserve all that was best of the old way of life. Memphians could still be citi-

6. Orgill to Albert Gore, Feb. 12, 1951, Orgill, "Manuscript Speech," Orgill Papers; Meeman, "Autobiography."

zens of Memphis and Shelby County and Tennessee and the U.S.A. but, in addition, they would be citizens of the larger Union of the Free and vote for representatives for the legislative and executive branches of the Union of the Free. "We are bound to have some kind of world government sooner or later," Orgill said. "Therefore, we ought to be figuring out the kind which will most surely preserve our individual freedom and what we call the American way of life. I hope this will be done while there is time to arrest Communism and prevent another war, rather than wait until Communism and another war force us to do it."[7]

Not only in Memphis but across the nation, people began to hear Edmund Orgill's plea for federalism. As Clarence Streit later reported, "a man in San Francisco came up to me after a speech and said, 'I have been hearing a lot about this idea already. There's a hardware man in Memphis, Tennessee, named Orgill. Every time we talk business on the phone, he keeps telling me about Atlantic Union.'" In Tennessee, Orgill organized a state chapter of Federal Union. In Louisville, Kentucky, he attended a regional meeting of Federal Union and was elected chairman of the eighteen-state regional meeting. He even converted Crump's congressman, Cliff Davis, who admitted: "Ed Orgill . . . got hold of me and gave me a real talking to. Ed almost prayed with me, and I finally said, 'Ed, you've converted me.'"[8]

While Orgill promoted Federal Union, two other Memphis advocates of federalism, Burch and Meeman, were attracted to a senate campaign that promised to weaken Edward Crump's political power. In 1948, Crump was attempting to drop the junior senator from Tennessee, Tom Stewart, and replace him with Judge John Mitchell. But Senator Stewart refused to withdraw from the race. The organization voters in the state might well divide between Mitchell and Stewart, enabling a third candidate—Estes Kefauver—to carry the election. Kefauver, a liberal congressman from Chattanooga, certainly had a chance if he could win strong support in Shelby County,

7. Clarence K. Streit, "Two Eds that Think as One," *Freedom and Union* 21 (Feb. 1966), 3–5; *Memphis Press-Scimitar,* Nov. 24, Dec. 22, 1947, Jan. 20, Feb. 4, 1948, March 6, 1950.
8. *Memphis Press-Scimitar,* Sept. 9, 1949.

where the local organization usually cast an overwhelming vote for Crump's candidate.

Meeman and Burch plotted a local Kefauver campaign around Edmund Orgill. They believed that any campaign needed a respected and distinguished member of the Memphis establishment to head the local campaign if Kefauver's candidacy were to have credibility. Orgill was their one acquaintance whose support might be worth 50,000 votes and the election for Estes Kefauver. The endorsement of the respected business leader would weaken Crump's hold over local voters, they believed, and encourage people all across Tennessee to believe that Estes could beat the machine. To secure Orgill's endorsement, careful planning seemed essential. Burch told Meeman and Kefauver, "Edmund is a man who makes up his own mind; you can't force him or push him." The two Memphians advised Kefauver that he must make himself more attractive to Orgill, and so the candidate visited Clarence Streit. He offered to sponsor a congressional resolution calling for a federal convention of the democracies. The grateful Streit then wrote to Orgill urging that he support Kefauver.[9]

Kefauver also sent Burch a personal endorsement of Federal Union, saying:

> During the nights I was sitting with my mother at the hospital in Knoxville I read *Union Now* from "kiver to kiver"—some parts I read again. I am entirely sold and tremendously impressed. I have thought the matter through from every angle, and I feel this is the plan we must go ahead with. It is . . . a splendid opportunity for somebody to make a full dress speech on the floor of the Senate or of the House about the whole problem, and it is the kind of thing that I want to do if I can get into the Senate.[10]

Burch sent Kefauver's note to Edmund Orgill along with his own persuasive statement:

> This is the golden opportunity for those of us who want to bring about the ultimate political crystallization of the sublime idea in which

9. Clarence Streit to Orgill, April 18, 1949; Meeman, "Autobiography," Meeman Papers.

10. Lucius Burch, Jr. to Orgill, May 14, 1948; Burch to Meeman, May 14, 1948, Meeman Papers.

we all believe so much. It is a matter of comparative insignificance whether you are preeminent in the hardware industry or whether I become and remain an outstanding lawyer. It *is* of tremendous importance to have even a small part in the accomplishment of the grand plan for which the world has remained in need for so many centuries. Clarence Streit has done more than anyone else to define and disseminate the idea and to prepare the minds of men for action. He and men of his type cannot carry the matter much further. To obtain the goal political action is necessary. This requires men in office who are forthright and courageous enough to march ahead of the thinking of the masses. Estes Kefauver is such a man and I do not believe I am overstating the matter to say that it rests within your power to achieve his election to the Senate.

If you will undertake this great work, I will help in any way I can. As you know, I am vulnerable to political reprisal through my clients and I do not enjoy either your financial independence or the immunity which you have by reason of the solid body of public opinion which will support you in any action you take. . . . Will you please commune with your conscience on this matter and, when I return, let me know if you have decided to pick up the gauntlet which opportunity has cast before you. You will find there are many whose opinions you respect and value who will stand staunchly in the vanguard with you. . . .

No more noble a work can be conceived than to establish a system and order through which [the little children] will be protected from the anticipated and yet undreamed-of terrors of the future. Second only to successful accomplishment is *to have made the attempt:* at least as we grow older we can say:

> What I aspired to be
> And was not, comforts me.

I have little doubt that we will have the excitement and satisfaction of success if we set our hands to this work but, if we do not, it is no reproach but rather the highest compliment that our reach exceeded our grasp. What I am trying to say is that since our self-respect will be increased by making the fight we are bound to be winners. Whatever the result, the only way to lose is not to try.[11]

Orgill was permitted one uninterrupted week for deliberation, and then Burch arranged a meeting with Orgill, Kefauver, Meeman, and himself. At this meeting on June 3 in the Hotel Peabody, Estes Kefauver reaffirmed his support of Federal Union and also explained his vote against the Taft-Hartley labor law. Although the

11. *Ibid.*

group disagreed with Kefauver's pro-union vote, they did admire his sincerity and forthright defense of his principles. Meeman challenged Orgill, "How can you go on making speeches for Federal Union if you don't step out and try to elect a senator who will advocate your plan?" Burch added, "Edmund, I'm going to come out for Estes, whatever the cost, whether you do or not."[12]

Orgill's reluctance to endorse Kefauver had nothing to do with fear of the Crump machine. His position in Memphis had so insulated him from insecurity that he did not really believe the stories of intimidation by the Crump organization. He even had a cordial speaking relationship with Mr. Crump, who had attended the wedding of Mrs. Orgill's parents and who loved to reminisce about it when Edmund occasionally saw him about civic affairs. Crump had once offered the chairmanship of the Shelby County Board of Education, but Orgill had declined the appointment and remained faithful to the family tradition of avoiding politics. To break a family tradition was difficult, but finally he decided that he must endorse Estes Kefauver and enter politics to make the Federal Union movement effective.[13]

Orgill was the fifth distinguished Memphian whom Edward Meeman and Lucius Burch had recruited to take a stand against Crump's candidate. They were all men of unimpeachable integrity whom E. H. Crump could never discredit by his favorite broadside smear —a newspaper ad as libelous as the law would allow.

J. Charles Poe was the first Memphian to tell Meeman, "I'm going to come out for Estes Kefauver."[14] Poe had been a newspaperman in Chattanooga and a personal friend of Kefauver; in fact, Estes had been his lawyer. Poe's journalistic interest in forestry had led him to the Tennessee Commission on Conservation and then to a vice-presidency of Nickey Brothers Lumber Company in Memphis, where he headed one of the first large-scale tree farming operations in the South. Poe and Meeman invited 100 independent voters to

12. Meeman, "Autobiography"; Burch to Orgill, May 27, 1948, Meeman Papers.
13. Interview with Edmund Orgill, July 13, 1973.
14. Meeman to Charles G. Neese, Jan. 3, 1948, Meeman Papers; *Memphis Press-Scimitar,* Jan. 19, Aug. 7, 1948.

meet Estes Kefauver at the Peabody Hotel on January 18. At that meeting Charles Poe publicly announced his support for Kefauver.

Dr. Henry B. Gotten was a prominent physician and a professor at the University of Tennessee Medical School who committed himself because of a past obligation to Edward Meeman. When Gotten, as secretary of the Memphis and Shelby County Medical Society, had been unable to reform the corrupt and inefficient Baptist Hospital, where the administration made beds available only for doctors who were friends and cronies, he had turned to Edward Meeman. A successful crusade in the *Press-Scimitar* caused the hospital administrator to resign, the board of trustees to reorganize, and the hospital charter to be rewritten. This assistance in reform so obligated Dr. Gotten that when Meeman later explained his need for a few distinguished Memphians to stand up and stop Crump's reign of fear, Dr. Gotten did not refuse even though he had no real interest in politics.[15] On January 22 the *Press-Scimitar* carried on its front page the story that Dr. Gotten announced his support of Kefauver.

Ed Dalstrom, manager of Graham Paper Company, had long taken an active interest in politics and never supported the Crump organization. Dalstrom had set out from his native Sweden to travel around the world in 1906, but he met an American engineer's daughter and settled down as a Memphis paper salesman. The sober Swedish-American surely seemed more like a minister than a salesman, and his concern for fairness took him into interracial causes—the Urban League and the board of directors of LeMoyne College. Dalstrom became a friend of Meeman through the Unitarian Church, which both attended, and through their common interest in Federal Union, which Dalstrom saw as essential for preserving the free enterprise system from communism.[16]

And there was William Barr, the self-made businessman who had been sales manager of the local De Soto Paint and Varnish Company, became a lieutenant colonel in the army and came out of the service with a patent on a non-inflammable paint remover, Klean

15. Henry B. Gotten, "Mud, Mules and Molasses," *The Egyptians* (1967), 51–71; *Memphis Press-Scimitar,* Jan. 22, 1948, Dec. 5, 1955; interview with Dr. Gotten, Aug. 30, 1973.

16. Interview with Edwin Dalstrom, June 20, 1973.

Strip. He successfully launched his own manufacturing business, W.M. Barr and Company, and then told his friends, "I didn't serve for democracy in World War II to come back and lose democracy at home." Barr announced his endorsement of Kefauver on page one of the *Press-Scimitar,* "I'm 100 percent for him. He is the type of fellow I'd like to see in Washington during the next few years. Foreign affairs are going to be extremely important. I think we need men like Estes Kefauver in the Senate handling them."[17]

The five met in Lucius Burch's office on the morning of June 10 to make a joint statement endorsing Estes Kefauver. But the final decision was difficult. Crump seemed to have known their plans. That very day, a full-page newspaper advertisement charged that Kefauver had been "the darling of the Communists" and had voted with the "ox-blood red Communist Congressman," Vito Marcantonio. The newspaper smear, with its implication that no patriotic American could vote for Estes, so distressed Orgill and Dalstrom that, despite assurances from Charles Poe—who said, "I knew him in Chattanooga and I know he is not a red"—the two insisted on calling Kefauver and securing an explanation of his voting with Marcantonio. Kefauver was located, and he explained that radical Marcantonio usually voted with the Democratic majority. Having satisfied themselves about Kefauver's defense, the group could have drafted a statement in time for the evening *Press-Scimitar.* But when Meeman arrived for the statement at noon, he was frankly and somewhat insultingly told by Edmund Orgill that the endorsement would have to appear first in the *Commercial Appeal.* Meeman's paper did not carry as much weight in the community, he was told, because he had so frequently gone off "half-cocked." Edward Meeman swallowed hard on being denied a banner headline story but accepted the decision of his hard-boiled friends.[18] The committee that had been his own was now surely dominated instead by Edmund Orgill.

17. *Memphis Press-Scimitar,* March 5, 1964.
18. Joseph Bruce Gorman, *Kefauver: A Political Biography* (New York: Oxford Univ. Press, 1971); interview with Edwin Dalstrom, June 20, 1973; interview with Dr. Henry B. Gotten, Aug. 30, 1973; interview with Edmund Orgill, July 13, 1973; *Memphis Press-Scimitar,* June 10, 1948.

On June 11 the *Commercial Appeal* carried the Kefauver endorsement, which began:

> The greatest problem before any citizen of Memphis, as it is of every American, is to prevent World War III. This can be done by making America strong and by perfecting adequate international organization. Estes Kefauver, by his record in Congress, has shown that he knows how to work for these objectives intelligently and effectively.[19]

The Orgill group intended to avoid campaigning against the Crump organization by simply stressing the necessity of electing a statesman who could help prevent war. But even though the Orgill group never mentioned Mr. Crump, the old boss was unwilling to permit such political independence. He called the home office of Graham Paper Company in St. Louis and unsuccessfully sought to have Dalstrom instructed to keep out of politics. Crump's emissary visited Lucius Burch's chief client, the Illinois Central Railroad, to point out the possible error of retaining an attorney who could not get along with the city administration. The Illinois Central officials refused to fire Burch and even stated that as long as he performed his legal work satisfactorily, the railroad would not interfere with his politics.[20]

Unable to intimidate these five men—they were above influence and had in their past no scandal that might be exposed—Crump turned to others who joined the Orgill group. When Mrs. Frances Coe became office manager for the Memphis campaign, Mr. Crump called her father, a prominent local businessman, to denounce him furiously for being unable to control his Vassar-educated daughter.[21] A liberal Northern education surely contributed to making a political activist; Mrs. Coe and the two other local women who agreed to work for Kefauver had all attended Vassar which, unlike Southern schools, emphasized the woman's obligation to participate in community affairs. Fresh from college in the 1930s, Mrs. Coe had become a board member of the most liberal women's group in town,

19. *Commercial Appeal,* June 11, 1948.
20. Interview with Lucius E. Burch, Jr., Sept. 23, 1973.
21. Interview with Mrs. Frances E. Coe, Mississippi Valley Collection; interview with Mrs. Coe, June 25, 1974.

the Young Women's Christian Association, and persuaded the YWCA to integrate by 1940. In addition to marrying into an old cotton family and mothering three daughters, she was active in the local Public Affairs Forum and won the respect of Edward Meeman, who asked her to join his group supporting Kefauver. Frances Coe was not intimidated by Mr. Crump, and she contributed much to the revolt against the machine.

The lumberman O.D. Bratton joined because he detested the Crump pressure tactics he had seen during his ten years in Memphis. When he did so, he received a phone call from his banker, a vice-president of Union Planters, asking him to drop the anti-Crump campaign.[22]

When Charles Pool became co-chairman of Southwestern Students for Kefauver, a family friend advised the young Catholic student, "I don't want to see you hurt yourself. I've talked about you with Harry Pierotti of the Knights of Columbus who has mentioned you to Crump. You're on the way up the ladder, if you don't announce for Kefauver." Other family friends warned Pool to consider that he was endangering his parent's property by alienating the Crump administration, which might retaliate through its inspectors and tax assessors. Local tax men appraised so erratically or maliciously that a piece of property might be listed in the tax books for any price from 20 to more than 100 percent of its market value. Crump's opponents who compared real estate assessments were likely to learn that their property had the highest assessment in the neighborhood.[23]

The great fear of the political organization emerged so plainly as to shock the previously nonpolitical Orgill and Gotten. They came face to face with the prejudice, intolerance, and abusive power of the boss. Orgill now confessed that previously he "had no realization of the depth and extent of the fear which existed here." Years later, Dr. Gotten could still recall one of his friends explaining, with

22. Interview with O.D. Bratton, Sept. 21, 1973.
23. Interview with Charles Pool, May 23, 1973; Civic Research Committee, "Report of the Local Tax Structure Study Committee on Real Estate Assessments in the City of Memphis" (Memphis, Tenn.: CRC, 1957) (mimeographed); W.H. Brandon to Edmund Orgill, March 7, 1958, CRC Papers, Mississippi Valley Collection.

tears streaming down his face, that he had wanted to support Kefauver, but his own mother was on the local school board. Former acquaintances no longer talked when they met Gotten on the street.[24]

Crump did not initiate every act of intimidation and pressure, but he certainly established the climate by labeling Kefauver a Red and then proposing that Edward J. Meeman get out of town because he had endorsed Kefauver. The attack on Meeman came in a radio broadcast (read for Crump by Mayor Pleasants) denouncing Kefauver as a Communist sympathizer and then announcing:

> I now propose that the Chamber of Commerce or some other body appoint a committee of seven . . . to go into the charges I have made against Kefauver's record—probe them to the bottom.
>
> If Meeman can prove through any reliable committee selected that these charges are false, I will get my hat and leave Memphis, never to return. On the other hand, if he cannot disprove these charges, then he will leave Memphis never to return.
>
> I have much at stake—home, family, children, grandchildren, many relatives, and I hope many friends; business and a great love and affection for the people of Memphis and Shelby County.
>
> Meeman lives outside the city, only has a sister and a brother, I understand, no relatives, no business of his own, what friends, I do not know. . . .
>
> Let's have a showdown on this challenge. Staggering facts. No side-stepping. No more twisting and turning of the truth. No glossing over.[25]

Estes Kefauver shrewdly turned the attack against Crump by announcing "I do not want E. H. Crump to have to take his family and move from Memphis, nor do I want Meeman to leave. It is a dictatorship indeed that cannot tolerate two men of different opinions. That's Joe Stalin's way, it's not my way."[26] Kefauver then offered to debate Crump's candidate, John Mitchell, on the issue "Is Estes Kefauver a Communist or a Communist Sympathizer?" but Crump had no interest in such a public debate.

Fear of Crump continued to keep the Kefauver group small. At

24. Edmund Orgill to Frank G. Clement, Aug. 13, 1952; Lucius Burch, Jr. to Lydel Sims, Aug. 21, 1952, Orgill Papers; interview with Dr. Gotten, Aug. 30, 1973.
25. *Commercial Appeal,* July 8, 1948.
26. *Ibid.*

the noon meetings of local campaign workers, Meeman would look over the tiny group in the Peabody Hotel and say, "Surely, surely, there are more people in Memphis who believe in freedom and honesty in elections than this."

Organized labor did join the Orgill-Meeman group. Industrial unions had no interest in Federal Union but supported Kefauver enthusiastically as a friend of labor who had voted against the Taft-Hartley Act. Because all their previous local labor campaigns against Crump candidates had failed, union men asked to work with the Orgill group in hopes of increasing their political effectiveness. Industrial unions had grown rapidly over the preceding decade as factory jobs expanded with four large industrial plants—International Harvester, Kimberly-Clark, Borg-Warner, and General Electric—built in Memphis after the war. While less than 7 percent of the local working force had industrial jobs in 1940, ten years later almost 20 percent worked in manufacturing. The CIO recruited its membership from the new industrial workers and had always been bitter against the Crump organization, which had attempted to drive the union out of town.

The Crump organization had feared that a successful CIO would make Memphis less attractive for industrial expansion. This concern for economic growth is revealed by Mayor Overton's note to Crump in 1937: "I am afraid Firestone won't expand much here if CIO gets busy. We will have to form a definite policy of some kind. Have you any suggestion?" Apparently Crump endorsed an unqualified resistance to the CIO and encouraged Mayor Overton to announce: "Imported CIO agitators, communists and highly paid professional organizers are not wanted in Memphis. They will not be tolerated." The verbal attack was followed by physical assaults upon Norman Smith, a CIO organizer, driving him from Memphis. Firestone remained free from unionization for several years as Crump's anti-industrial unionism continued and the available pool of Mid-South workers continued to provide hundreds of eager white applicants for the forty-cent-an-hour jobs and blacks for the thirty-two-cent-an-hour jobs.[27]

27. Watkins Overton to E. H. Crump, Aug. 13, 1937, Watkins Overton Papers, Box 2, Mississippi Valley Collection; Lucy Randolph Mason, *To Win These Rights: A Personal History of the CIO in the South* (New York: Harper, 1952), 104–5.

R. H. Routon, who later became the CIO spokesman at Firestone, had been one of 300 anxious job seekers who lined up outside Firestone office on the cold, rainy morning of January 3, 1938. Arriving at 4:00 A.M., he secured the ninth place in the line and four chilling hours later had scarcely been interviewed before the personnel office closed the line and sent all the remaining men home. The newly hired Routon and his fellow workers felt themselves extremely fortunate to have the industrial jobs even though Firestone "worked the hell out of them" and paid only half the wages earned in the company's plant in Akron, Ohio. While neither low pay nor exhausting work turned the workers against the company, management brutality produced unionization. On August 29, 1940, while CIO organizer George R. Bass distributed union literature in front of the plant, more than a score of Firestone supervisors assaulted him with pipes and chains while Routon and several hundred other employees watched.[28]

The Bass incident lost the anti-union campaign for Firestone. Although the Crump organization temporarily blocked the CIO for another year by pushing the friendly American Federation of Labor to organize Firestone, the workers finally voted to switch from the AFL to the CIO. Crump still did not give up easily. He sent for the new local president of the CIO, R. H. Routon, having him brought to Crump's insurance office in a police squad car. "We aren't going to have any CIO nigger unions in Memphis," Crump asserted. "They can do what they want in Detroit, Chicago and New York City, but we aren't going to have it in Memphis."[29]

Routon might have been more easily intimidated if he had been a Memphian familiar with machine power, but his upbringing in a small Southern town had made him hostile to urban machines and certain of his high school civic lessons about bosses and democracy. He had learned unionism from his father, a railroad man, had witnessed the exploitation of labor, and had gained courage from reading Irving Stone's *Attorney for the Defense,* a biography of Clarence Darrow, who had boldly defended labor against local power

28. Interview with R. H. Routon, April 3, 1974; *Commercial Appeal,* Aug. 30, 1940.
29. *Ibid.*

elites. So now that Routon spoke for his fellow workers at Firestone he never hesitated to stand up to Crump and insist that the CIO was in Memphis to stay.

The Boss slammed his fist down hard enough to rattle the gold-plated telephone on his desk, his bushy eyebrows quivered like a minor earth tremor, and he roared, "I say we are not going to have it."

"I say we are," Routon replied.

"That's all I have to say to you," Crump concluded abruptly.

President Franklin Roosevelt sent a special investigator from the Justice Department to probe Shelby County violations of civil rights following the beating of George Bass, and the Crump organization seemed to avoid physical pressure thereafter. Routon suffered no more than a couple of harassing arrests even though he boldly moved on to head the local CIO political action committee, teaching Firestone workers to become qualified and informed voters. Routon placed poll watchers in more than half the voting precincts in the 1946 political campaign against the Crump machine, and while his CIO forces lost heavily in their first effort to defeat Crump's Senator K. D. McKellar and Governor James McCord, they learned election tactics, witnessed voting irregularities, and developed a burning desire to beat Crump in the next election.[30]

Routon and the CIO had fought virtually alone in 1946, but two years later the conservative AFL, which had traditionally been controlled by Crump men, had little choice but to endorse Estes Kefauver because he had voted pro-union against the Taft-Hartley Act. Routon would gladly work with the AFL and even with the wealthy businessmen against Crump. He asked the Meeman group if labor could join them in a united front, and so the vice-president of the local AFL Trades and Labor Council, Frank B. Miles, and the CIO representative, R. H. Routon, joined the Memphis committee for Kefauver and shared their practical political experience and their union workers in the campaign to break Crump's power.

A separate Kefauver organization operated in black Memphis under the wealthy insurance executive Dr. J. E. Walker, with whom

30. *Ibid.*; Mason, *To Win These Rights,* 109–13; *Commercial Appeal,* Aug. 2, 1946.

Orgill and Dalstrom had worked in past Community Fund drives. The black campaign kept in touch with the white but was financially self-supporting and, of course, more concerned with civil rights than Federal Union. Boss Crump had recently antagonized local blacks by refusing to permit the Freedom Train to stop in Memphis with its display of patriotic documents because the train sponsors would not allow visitors to be segregated by race. In addition to barring the Freedom Train from Memphis, Crump and his senatorial candidate denounced President Harry Truman and the Democratic civil rights program. Crump broke with the Democratic party and supported the Dixiecrats, asserting, "I would be willing to go to jail and stay there the balance of my life rather than abide by it [civil rights]. . . . In his [Truman's] scheming, cold-blooded effort to outdo Henry Wallace and Governor Dewey of New York for the Negro vote, he has endeavored to reduce the South to a country of crawling cowards." By contrast, Estes Kefauver's endorsement of one Truman goal—abolition of the poll tax—made him appear more liberal and perhaps suggested that he would later become a full supporter of civil rights for blacks. So the handful of black capitalists enthusiastically joined the CIO and the Orgill group in campaigning for Kefauver.[31]

With the cooperation of blacks, labor, and Meeman's friends, Memphis seemed to be emerging from the old closed society. The population of the city had grown by a third during the last decade, to almost 400,000, and the new Memphians were surely less indebted to the old machine. To reach these voters and to illustrate that no one need fear to speak out in disagreement with Crump, the Orgill group delivered speeches all across Memphis, in backyards and church lawns, over sound trucks and radio. They emphasized that the election of a United States senator should be above local politics if the American way of life were to be preserved. Kefauver was the most qualified statesman, author of a highly regarded book, *Twentieth Century Congress* (1947), and the choice of *Collier's* magazine as one of the ten best representatives. Certainly Ke-

31. Tucker, *Lieutenant Lee of Beale Street,* 146; *Memphis Press-Scimitar,* Nov. 18, 1947, March 2, 1948; interview with Mrs. Coe, Mississippi Valley Collection.

fauver was no Communist. "I am attorney for a number of large corporations," Lucius Burch said, "would I vote for a Communist? Mr. Edmund Orgill runs one of the biggest businesses in Memphis, Orgill Brothers, and Mr. O.D. Bratton runs a number of large lumber mills. These men are employers and businessmen. Would men of this type vote for a Communist?"[32]

Persuading voters to support Kefauver was only half the battle. More important was to secure an honest ballot count. In some past elections, the voting results had been changed after the ballots were cast. Now the promise of a fair election seemed essential if those Memphians who had been disillusioned with the system could be persuaded to vote at all. Rumors of FBI poll watchers were spread. Lucius Burch prepared a digest of election laws and the League of Women Voters, whose Memphis members were Kefauver supporters, organized "Schools for Watchers". On election day Crump's city and county employees, who ran the election machinery, were better watched than ever before by middle-class women, businessmen, and union members.[33]

Election day delighted workers for Kefauver. In new suburban neighborhoods on the eastern fringe of the city, such as National Cemetery precinct, newcomers turned out to vote against Crump's candidate. As one distressed Crump ward heeler lamented, "I thought I knew the people who lived out here, but I've never seen as many strange people in my life, and I can tell the way they're looking at me that they're not for us. We are really getting clobbered out here." The heavily white labor precinct of Frayser, populated by CIO Firestone rubber workers, Ford assembly employees belonging to United Auto Workers' locals, and AFL construction, streetcar, and railroad men, voted 55 percent for Kefauver. In black precincts some ballots were still marked for the voter by Crump election workers, but Kefauver poll watchers stopped much of this illegal voting, and in three predominately black precincts the majority actually went for Kefauver. White Memphians were more rebellious than black Memphians. Crump had never lost a city voting box

32. *Commercial Appeal,* July 24, 29, 30, 1948.
33. Interview with O.D. Bratton, Sept. 21, 1973; interview with Charles Pool, May 23, 1973; interview with Dr. Henry B. Gotten, Aug. 30, 1973.

since 1926, but this time he lost twenty-four precincts. The Crump candidate still carried Shelby County with 37,000 votes to Kefauver's 27,000, but that was too few to undermine Kefauver's state-wide victory margin, which shattered Crump's supremacy over Tennessee politics.[34]

The fear that had compelled obedience to the Crump machine now released its grip on Memphians. No political organization ever again looks so intimidating after it loses its friends in state and national government (Gordon Browning defeated Crump's candidate, Jim McCord, for governor of Tennessee, and President Harry Truman won reelection despite Crump's opposition). Without friends in high places, E. H. Crump would not dare retaliate against those leading Memphians who had stood up and declared their independence. In fact, Crump now abandoned the stick completely and extended the carrot by hiring the first black policeman in order to please the Negro community. He retired his hatchet man, Will Gerber, who had denounced the independents, replaced his mayor, James E. Pleasants, and included a CIO leader in his next slate of state legislative candidates.[35] Crump would shrewdly perpetuate his local political organization, but it could never again exercise dictatorial power.

Although Kefauver's campaign diverted the attention of Orgill's group from the Federal Union to political bossism, the middle-class reformers remained committed to a federation of the Western democracies. Senator Kefauver sponsored a congressional Atlantic Union Resolution in 1949, repaying his Memphis election debt. The Orgill chapter of Federal Union grew to 300 members—Memphians who believed that the North Atlantic Treaty Organization and the Marshall Plan were not enough to protect the world from Russian Communism. The energy and commitment of the Memphis chapter won prominent mention in 1950 when *Time* magazine published a

34. Charles Edmundson, "How Kefauver Beat Crump," *Harpers* 198 (Jan. 1949), 78–84; Gorman, *Kefauver,* 55–61; *Commercial Appeal,* Aug. 7, 1948; in the three-cornered race, incumbent Senator Tom Stewart received 118,000 votes; Kefauver thus received a plurality rather than a clear majority.

35. *Memphis Press-Scimitar,* Aug. 26, Sept. 10, 1948; *Commercial Appeal,* July 6, 1950.

cover story about Clarence Streit. When Streit organized the first Atlantic Union Congress in 1951, he awarded the convention to Memphis. Eight years later, when the Atlantic Congress met in London, Edmund Orgill and Edward Meeman were delegates. Even though Orgill, Meeman, and Lucius Burch joined other causes, their commitment to Atlantic Union remained a vital concern. And certainly, without Edmund Orgill's original commitment to Federal Union, he would never have become a part of the anti-Crump reform movement in Memphis.[36]

36. *Freedom and Union* 4 (September 1948), 2–6; *Time* 55 (March 27, 1950); *Memphis Press-Scimitar,* July 26, 1949, Nov. 1–3, 1951.

4.

The Citizens Study Group

Kefauver's victory put a Federal Union advocate in the Senate but did not fully liberate Shelby County. Even though freedom of speech had returned and a few Memphians now felt unrestrained enough to boo Crump's name at a baseball game, the majority did not feel free to vote against his candidates. City and county employees were not absolved from machine instructions to contribute and to work in political campaigns. Memphians were not even free from suspicions that ballot boxes could still be manipulated by the political organization. The Meeman coalition had put the machine on the defensive, but to insure the continued growth of political freedom at home, a permanent local reform organization would be necessary.[1]

While the Federal Union advocates talked of organizing a civic reform group, a surprise protest of city policemen angered by low wages and arbitrary dismissals provided an occasion to press for a civil service law that would make merit and not political service the guarantee of continued employment. A reformers' committee of young attorneys, Bailey Brown, Lewis R. Donelson III, Francis Loring, James M. Manire, W. Wright Mitchell, Jr., and Albert C.

1. *Commercial Appeal,* Aug. 7, 1948; interview with O. D. Bratton, Sept. 21, 1973; interview with Dr. Henry B. Gotten, Aug. 30, 1973.

Rickey, Jr., drafted a model civil service law which was debated and endorsed by 500 citizens opposing Crump who met with the Orgill group in the Chisca Hotel Ballroom. Orgill voiced the determination of the assembled Memphians: "If democracy is to succeed, more citizens are going to have to take an interest in civic affairs. It is our duty and our obligation." Faced with this public display of opposition, the Crump organization gave the Memphis police their salary increase and a civil service law which required employee dismissals to be approved by a civil service commission rather than by the police commissioner. However, Crump refused to outlaw the old practice of requiring city employees to engage in political work.[2]

Winning even a limited civil service law encouraged the more cautious reformers, who advocated a research and study group rather than a political organization which would put up candidates for office. The bolder political activists, led by Edward Meeman, hoped to campaign directly against the political machine in every election. The prudent Lucius Burch and Edmund Orgill, who believed it folly to "charge the cannon mouth," preferred to organize a study group that would promote government reforms and avoid direct political action against Crump. Since none of the civic leaders had the political ambition to cultivate a personal following or to subject himself to the unpleasantness of political attack, a research and educational organization seemed preferable. If Memphians were to be led back into democratic politics, they needed first to begin discussing the issues, a step that they would fear to take if the discussion leaders outwardly opposed Crump. As Edmund Orgill put it: "I think that it will hurt the effectiveness of this committee, if we are constantly referred to as the faction opposed to Mr. Crump."[3] A study group, it was agreed, would gain far more community trust if it advertised itself as an organization of citizens interested in public affairs and willing to support all ideas for good government, even Mr. Crump's. Publicizing nonpartisan solutions for municipal problems would

2. *Memphis Press-Scimitar,* Nov. 23, 1948; *Commercial Appeal,* Nov. 18, 23, Dec. 23, 1948.
3. Edmund Orgill to Harry Woodbury, June 14, 1949, Civic Research Committee Papers, Mississippi Valley Collection.

create a popular following, the reformers thought, and surely the practical politicians would then endorse the proposals.

Edward Meeman did not object to organizing a study group; in fact, he had been advocating one for years.[4] As a long-time member of the National Municipal League, which advocated both an educational group and a political action group for every community, Meeman protested that his friends were enacting only half the civic program that had proven effective in deposing bosses and establishing good government in other cities. But Meeman was outvoted, and the reformers organized only an educational group—the Civic Research Committee (CRC). The new committee made its first statement in May 1949, emphasizing that "in no sense may either the committee or its participating members be designated as anti-administration."[5] Crump's leading official, Mayor Watkins Overton, was even invited to serve on a subcommittee, but the mayor refused to cooperate and bitterly denounced the new organization as "a strictly political move to discredit the city government."[6]

The fifty charter members of Civic Research included leaders of the local AFL and the CIO, but most were those upper-class moralists who traditionally assume leadership in condemning corruption and inefficiency in American cities. They included housewives active in the American Association of University Women and the Vassar Club, independent physicians, attorneys, and businessmen who had been active in Federal Union and the Kefauver campaign. Aggressive recruiting brought in 250 more middle-class independents within a year, but leadership remained with the organizers who took places on the five-man executive board of CRC and named committees to work toward council-manager government, city-county consolidation, voting machines, and permanent voter registration. The Orgill group also provided much of the financing by making $500 contributions, while the more typical dues were two-dollar member-

4. Lucius Burch, Jr. to Edward Meeman, Aug. 28, 1946, Meeman Papers.

5. *Commercial Appeal,* May 28, 1949.

6. Burch to Watkins Overton, July 22, 1949, Box 6, Overton Papers; Overton had been invited back by Crump's organization as head of the board of education and then, in 1949, to become mayor again.

ships. The money went for speakers, office expenses, and an able executive secretary, Charles Pool, who had earned an M.A. in history and was studying for a degree in law.[7]

Although its charter prohibited the study group from engaging in politics, two Meeman activists on the board—lumberman O.D. Bratton and realtor Gilmer Richardson—could not be discouraged from running for office. Richardson was a long-time critic of Crump who had observed massive voting fraud while serving as a poll watcher in 1932. "I saw votes cast for 632 persons who never came near the polls," he said. "I can prove that at any time. I have the proof." Richardson and Bratton were so eager to see challengers to Crump candidates who had been unopposed for twenty years in local elections that they and Ann Rickey, the wife of a young attorney, put up a slate of candidates to run against Crump's legislative ticket in 1950.[8] This Green-Light reform ticket was soundly trounced in the summer elections, demonstrating the point made by Burch and Orgill, that a great deal of election reform and educational work would be necessary before the machine could be beaten.

The Civic Research Committee restricted its involvement in racial issues just as it avoided direct political action. Race produced controversy, and the organization had no wish to make itself even more unpopular by taking a liberal stand on racial questions. But the group did accept black members after a couple of years, and two board members even publicly endorsed the candidacy of Dr. J.E. Walker, the black insurance executive who had worked with them in the Kefauver campaign, for the city school board in 1951. Both O.D. Bratton and Edmund Orgill spoke for Walker, with Orgill saying, "I really believe that it would be good . . . for Dr. Walker to be elected. . . . I think he is better qualified than the other candidates, and . . . it would give the Negroes a feeling that they were

7. Interview with Charles E. Pool, May 23, 1973; *Commercial Appeal,* May 28, June 21, 1949; Lorin Peterson, *The Day of the Mugwump* (New York: Random, 1961), 14–17, 206–7.

8. *Memphis Press-Scimitar,* June 23, July 26, 1950; *Commercial Appeal,* July 6, 30, 1950; Mrs. Frances E. Coe interview, Brister Library; the independent candidates were O.D. Bratton, Gilmer Richardson, Ann Rickey, C.W. Bond, Dolph Clark, James A. Welsh, E.W. Sprague, B. Ray Allen, T.A. Patterson, Howard Massey, and W.S. Douglass.

having a part in the operations of our school. This might lessen to some extent their insistence upon their children attending the same schools as white children."⁹ Orgill's endorsement brought complaints from white Mississippi hardware customers, but he stoutly defended his conservative support of Walker, a fellow CRC member. The Civic Research Committee itself, to be sure, never came out for school board integration. The white reformers had not won acceptance for their good government ideas and certainly were not going to hazard their chances by pushing integration beyond their own organization.

The CRC concentrated on taking the election machinery out of the hands of the Crump organization and achieved early success because the Tennessee anti-machine candidate, Gordon Browning, had been elected governor in 1948. Governor Browning promptly backed a series of state election reforms to end the Crump-manipulated poll tax and annual voter registration. The reformer's goal of permanent registration began. Governor Browning's legislation also prohibited public employees from serving as election officials, and the governor appointed three CRC members (Edmund Orgill, Gilmer Richardson, and Millsaps Fitzhugh) to the Shelby County Election Commission to carry out the election reforms. The entire CRC assisted by encouraging all Memphians to apply for their permanent voter registration and by working through the civic clubs to recruit volunteers to serve as election officials. Even though independents continued to lose elections after 1950, they could take some satisfaction in knowing that the vote count had been honest because election officials were no longer controlled by the Crump organization.[10]

Voting machines were still another means of securing honest elections, and the CRC lobbied for them. It applied pressure on local government by securing endorsements of voting machines from the

9. *Memphis Press-Scimitar,* Nov. 7, 1951; Orgill to Frank Ahlgren, Aug. 13, 1951; Orgill to Maury Leftwich, Nov. 21, 1951, Orgill Papers; interview with O. D. Bratton, Sept. 21, 1973.

10. Edmund Orgill, statement, Orgill Papers; Lucius Burch, Jr. to Frances Coe, March 6, 1953, Meeman Papers; *Memphis Press-Scimitar,* June 28, 1950; Crump recovered control of election machinery in 1953, following the victory of his candidate, Frank Clement, over Governor Gordon Browning.

press, labor, chamber of commerce, civic clubs, and more than fourteen thousand petition signers. Members of the study group appeared before city and county government explaining that voting machines had been in existence for fifty years and that most large cities had now ended the laborious task of counting ballots by hand and had turned to the swift and accurate voting machine. When Crump's reluctant officials hesitated to spend the half-million dollars for machines and referred the issue to the voters in 1952, Civic Research waged a successful campaign that persuaded Memphians to approve the expenditure by a five-to-one vote.[11]

The study group campaigned just as energetically and diligently to replace the Memphis commission government with a council-manager form but without the success won for their other government reforms. As members of the National Municipal League, the reformers knew the council-manager plan to be the fastest growing form of municipal government and the commission form the most frequently abandoned. Municipal authorities agreed that commission government, which formerly enjoyed a brief national popularity, had proven inefficient because both legislative and administrative functions were combined in five elected commissioners. The five officials constituted not only the legislative branch of the government; in addition, each headed one of the major divisions of city government and generally demonstrated little willingness to cooperate with the other four administrators. In Memphis, E. H. Crump had been able to keep the commissioners working as a team. But Crump was growing old, and it would be wise, Lucius Burch said, to adopt a form like the modern corporation, which could function effectively after the Boss was gone. Let the people elect a part-time council to make policy and hire a trained city manager to administer the government. "This is the simple way of making majority rule really work," Edmund Orgill agreed. "Policy makers are elected. Skilled administrators are appointed."[12]

11. *Commercial Appeal,* June 27, 1950; *Memphis Press-Scimitar,* Oct. 2, 1950; W. M. Barr to Mrs. Lawrence Coe, Aug. 11, 1950; Charles Pool to Civic Researchers, July 18, 1952, CRC Papers; Watkins Overton to Paul Barret, Nov. 13, 1950, Box 13, Overton Papers.

12. *Memphis Press-Scimitar,* Jan. 1, 1949; Lucius E. Burch, Jr., "Council-

To promote the manager-council form, Civic Research brought in speakers from Cincinnati, Des Moines, Kansas City, San Antonio, and Dallas, where good government functioned under that system. The committee also sought to interest the leaders of the local chamber of commerce in government reform. In many cities the business community promoted the council-manager form, but in Memphis the capitalists seemed reluctant to join a movement led by Kefauver liberals. Businessmen agreed that the old commission would no longer work after Crump passed on, but they did not want to consider the matter until then. The hesitation of businessmen frustrated Ed Meeman and caused him to urge Lucius Burch and Edmund Orgill to run for mayor as a means of publicizing the merits of council-manager government; but neither of the shrewd reformers wished to weaken his personal effectiveness by a losing political campaign. So the council-manager goal continued to be pursued by speeches, promotional literature, and personal evangelism.[13]

Although council-manager government remained a central concern, the study group began to devote more of its attention to city planning—the anticipation of public construction needs for the physical development of the city. The interest in city planning led to another criticism of Crump's leadership. While Memphis had exploded in population and physical size since the war, Mr. Crump sought to hold the line on expenses by delaying construction of necessary public roads and buildings. With a population then of 435,000, the city had mushroomed far beyond its old boundaries, which during the thirties, extended only four and one-half miles east from the central business district on the river bluff. By the fifties, new housing subdivisions leapfrogged each other ten miles east from downtown to White Station. North-south expansion of the population began spilling over the old swampy boundaries of the Wolf River on the north and Nonconnah Creek on the south. From

Manager Government as Related to Memphis, Tennessee," *The Egyptians* (1951), 49–59.

13. Meeman to Burch, July 31, 1951; Burch to Meeman, Aug. 6, 1951, Orgill to Meeman, Dec. 19, 1951, Meeman Papers; Orgill to Charles P. Taft, Aug. 18, 1949, Orgill Papers; *Commercial Appeal,* Oct. 2, 1949; *Memphis Press-Scimitar,* Nov. 28, 1949, March 19,1952, March 31, 1953.

the central business district, the Memphis population now resided two miles north, two miles south, and ten miles east. The suburban sprawl to the east was connected by Shelby County's old two-lane roads. Streets that had served 60,000 vehicles in 1940 were now choked by 140,000 cars, trucks, and buses. Traffic congestion encouraged retail decentralization, and in 1949 Poplar Plaza, the first shopping center, opened in the eastern suburbs, miles from the central business district. Downtown merchants were immediately troubled that their business would inevitably decline.[14]

The downtown business community organized against suburban shopping centers and traffic congestion by creating a Downtown Association and seeking city assistance for public parking garages, banning of parking on Main Street, and the construction of expressways for moving traffic rapidly across town. Mr. Crump gave little support to the downtown bankers, real estate men, and merchants, however; the city government even refused to help the association raise money for the parking garage. While the machine extended no aid to the community downtown, in 1952 the Civic Research Committee appointed its own planning committee of business and professional men—Bruckner Chase, E.D. Schumacher, Lucian Dent, and Tom Robinson—to study downtown transportation as well as all the other urban problems of growth, decay, and renewal.[15]

Memphis offered many examples of lack of planning even though Mr. Crump had considered himself to be a master planner. One case in point was the sewer system, which emptied its untreated contents into the Mississippi River. As the city moved east from the river in a narrow belt between the Wolf River on the north and Nonconnah Creek on the south, the new subdivisions and industries began dumping sewage into the smaller streams, turning them into open sewers that killed all wildlife and, more offensive to Memphians, spread foul odors for miles around. The Wolf emptied into the Mississippi River just below downtown Cossitt Library, and in the summer the whole central business district could smell the "stinking,

14. Harland Bartholomew and Associates, *Comprehensive Plan: Memphis, Tenn.* (St. Louis, Mo.: HBA, 1955), 1–11; *Memphis Press-Scimitar,* Oct. 15, 1952.
15. *Memphis Press-Scimitar,* Dec. 16, 1950, Jan. 30, 1953; *Commercial Appeal,* Sept. 15, 1952.

unsightly and odoriferous mess." Tennessee water pollution regulations had never applied to the Wolf because the law sought only to protect drinking water, and no one drank water from the Mississippi or the lower Wolf. Memphis was legally free to treat the streams as sewers. The Crump administration never considered sewage treatment plants at all. It regarded as too expensive the proposed construction of sewer mains to keep pollution out of the smaller streams and carry it directly into the Mississippi. Sewage policy consisted of little more than planning to ask the federal government to divert the mouth of Wolf River away from downtown Memphis.[16]

Crump remained so committed to having the lowest city taxes in the nation that he postponed needed capital improvements and metropolitan annexation. Memphis should have been planning to annex Frayser and Whitehaven, fringe communities that were growing up on the outskirts of Memphis and threatening the future expansion of the central city. Just north of Wolf River the community of Frayser, grown to 15,000, so needed a sewage system that the residents actively sought annexation by Memphis. When the city took no interest, they discussed incorporating themselves into a separate city. "City Hall is penny wise and pound foolish," Edward Meeman declared in the *Press-Scimitar* when Crump refused to annex Frayser because of the cost.[17]

Expressway planning was also neglected by the Crump administration. Other Southern cities such as Dallas, San Antonio, Houston, New Orleans, and Atlanta had begun constructing divided, limited access freeways for moving traffic rapidly through congested urban areas. The administration's disinterest in freeways angered the CRC city planning subcommittee that met weekly to discuss the needs of Memphis. "What are the city plans for express-

16. *Memphis Press-Scimitar,* Jan. 24, March 19, May 13, Oct. 13, 1952, Feb. 19, Oct. 15, 1953; Meeman's concern for conservation of natural resources was not fully shared by the civic planning committee concerned about the expressway; the interceptor sewer was finally begun in 1955 and completed in 1959 (*Memphis Press-Scimitar,* Oct. 21, 1959); sewage treatment did not begin until the 1970s. See Bergen S. Merrill, Jr. (ed.), *Memphis in the Seventies* (Memphis: Memphis State Univ., 1970), 176–80; *Commercial Appeal,* Jan. 7, 1973.
17. *Memphis Press-Scimitar,* June 30, Oct. 2, 13, 14, 1953, Feb. 19, 1954.

ways?" the subcommittee demanded of Mayor Watkins Overton in 1952 . Committee members attended the American Civic and Planning Association convention in March 1953 and returned with a plan to sell to the city government. The committee brought back the planning director of New Orleans, Louis Bisso, for a series of meetings with city officials. Bisso said that every modern city required a comprehensive plan, for expressways and every other municipal need, that only a professional urban planning and engineering firm could prepare. The Harland Bartholomew firm, which had prepared a city plan for Memphis in 1924, still had an excellent reputation, and Bisso urged that Memphis again hire Bartholomew.[18]

City Hall turned friendly and receptive to Civic Research after Mayor Watkins Overton resigned in February 1953. Overton, who had been restored to power by Mr. Crump in 1949, had bitterly opposed every reform idea. Overton and Crump were in perfect agreement that the reformers were dangerous political enemies, but the two old machine politicians soon ceased to agree about much else. Crump accused Overton of plotting with Bert Bates to build a rival political machine. After trading insults and waging an extended feud with the Boss, Overton finally quit in early 1953. He was replaced by Frank Tobey, a wise and congenial engineer who had worked as a city employee for thirty years.[19] Tobey readily approved city planning and managed to secure Mr. Crump's permission in June 1953 for the city to hire Bartholomew.

While Bartholomew prepared his study of Memphis, the *Press-Scimitar* and the Civic Research Committee continued to build public support for planning, showing civic clubs "The Living City," an educational film that explained the urban problems of development and blight and efforts by the citizens of Pittsburgh and Los Angeles to overcome them. The study group and Southwestern's Adult Educational Center, which had been offering seminars in city planning,

18. Minutes of CRC Planning Committee, Dec. 8, 1952, Jan. 22, 1953, CRC Papers; *Memphis Press-Scimitar,* Dec. 9, 10, 1952, Jan. 1, Feb. 24, April 29, June 19, 1953.

19. E. H. Crump to Bert Bates, Nov. 14, 1950, Box 13, Overton Papers; Overton Resignation Statement, Feb. 7, 1953, Box 9, Overton Papers; *Memphis Press-Scimitar,* Oct. 25, 1950, Feb. 7, 8, 13, 1951; *Commercial Appeal,* Dec. 4, 5, 7, 1952.

even produced their own television film series, "The City is You." It began with the origins of the city in history and continued, through nine Sunday afternoon programs, to explain the major goals of urban planning. The CRC planning publicity sought to persuade the citizens, and thus Mr. Crump, that the expensive public improvements recommended by the Bartholomew plan would be absolutely necessary. Even though Mayor Tobey supported city planning, he needed a great deal of support if Mr. Crump were to be persuaded to permit additional municipal spending.[20]

The Civic Research Committee found Mayor Tobey so open and willing to discuss city problems that they had no thought of opposing his election to a new term in 1955. The reformers, however, still objected to the old commission form of government and began quietly and successfully organizing business leaders for council-manager as Mr. Crump's heart weakened in the summer of 1954. Charles Pool, executive secretary of CRC, explained how the reformers won over the businessmen:

> Our main problem has been that people looked upon these independents as a liberal-labor Kefauver movement because CRC and political independence from Crump dominated politics . . . came about as a result of the 1948 Kefauver campaign. This stigma, of sorts, made the conservative business and professional elements leery of CRC, and of C-M [council-manager]. Therefore, it was the main task of C-M advocates to overcome this, and that has been done by playing up C-M as the businessman's type of government—i.e., . . . patterned after the corporation and giving the businessman a chance to participate actively and officially in city government, We now have some 50 or 75 leading business and professional men, I suppose, who have signed a statement —not yet released—endorsing C-M. . . . By Monday, these should be organized in a citizens committee for council-manager to be made public whenever the group thinks it feasible.[21]

The day after Crump's funeral, October 18, Orgill met with fellow council-manager advocates Edward Meeman, Roane Waring, Chuck Hutton, Caffee Robertson, Bill Barr, and George Grider.

---

20. *Memphis Press-Scimitar,* Oct. 6, 1952; Orgill to Twentieth Century Fund, Jan. 6, 1954, Laurence F. Kinney to Orgill, Jan. 6, 1954, CRC Papers; *Memphis Press-Scimitar,* March 5, 1954.
21. Charles Pool to Richard S. Childs, Oct. 15, 1954, CRC Papers.

They mapped out the formation of the Council-Manager Committee: an organization whose charter, unlike that of the CRC, would not prohibit engaging in political activity. The new group was organized by Civic Research members, but these reformers did not want the new committee associated with the CRC or a Kefauver group, so they turned the leadership over to a conservative Republican business executive, R. A. Trippeer. He would explain the council-manager movement as an effort for "insuring that the good things Mr. E. H. Crump left us are protected, continued, and expanded."[22]

The Council-Manager Committee supported Mayor Tobey's campaign for reelection. These reformers were strongly opposed to former mayor Watkins Overton, who wanted to return to politics now that Crump was gone and who had his own plans for changing the city government to a strong mayor-council form that would permit him to build his own political machine. When Mayor Tobey suffered a fatal heart attack in September 1955, during the campaign, Watkins Overton became the only candidate for mayor. The reformers felt compelled now to enter the political contest with a candidate of their own to prevent the restoration of machine government and to work for the goal of council-manager government.[23]

On September 27, the Council-Manager Committee met and reorganized itself as the Edmund Orgill for Mayor Committee. All agreed that Orgill should be their candidate. As a financially independent executive he could afford to retire from business and become a low-paid public official, but more important, he had the energy, drive, and confidence to take charge of city government. Orgill clearly was more conscientious than anyone else around, and although he lacked the charismatic ability to arouse emotion in crowds of people, he inspired his own acquaintances to follow almost anywhere he chose to lead. So friends drafted Edmund Orgill and would not allow him to refuse.[24]

22. *Memphis Press-Scimitar,* April 13, 21, 1954; Charles Pool to Alfred Willoughby, April 28, 1954, Pool to Richard S. Childs, Oct. 15, 1954, CRC Papers; George Grider to Dick Trippeer, Oct. 19, 1954, Orgill Papers; *Commercial Appeal,* Oct. 24, 1954.

23. *Memphis Press-Scimitar,* Sept. 12, 14, 1955.

24. Interview with Burch, Sept. 23, 1973; *Memphis Press-Scimitar,* Sept. 27, 1955; *Commercial Appeal,* Sept. 28, 1955.

Orgill entered the campaign assuming that the city commissioners would have their own candidate in the race, a candidate who would campaign for retention of the commission form of government, thus giving the voters a choice among three forms of government. Orgill's first speeches were council-manager addresses. But the old Crump organization failed to put up a third candidate, and so the election could not really be a referendum on the form of government. Opinion polls also revealed that voters had little interest in council-manager reform. The opinion analysis for Orgill explained that most voters looked at the election contest as one of personality: there would be no popular revolt against the traditional Shelby County machine or the commission government. The mood of the Memphis electorate, according to the opinion analysis, was a "desire to see an orderly adjustment to the fact that the Shelby County machine, as such, no longer exists; a desire to see the best features of that machine retained and the worst relegated to historical limbo. . . ."[25]

In the face of "scientific" opinion, the Orgill advisers agreed that their candidate should ease away from his announced efforts to change the form of government and agree to work and serve on the city commission until the voters wished a change. The thrust of the campaign, advisers agreed, should be an attack on Watkins Overton's lack of leadership. So Orgill reminded the voters that even though Overton had been mayor for many years, he had been only a "figurehead" while Mr. Crump had been the real leader. As a Crump official himself had once explained, "Mr. Crump is engineer, conductor and flagman. He runs the train—we are all tickled to death to ride." Overton had been tickled to ride Mr. Crump's train but had been so difficult to get along with that the Boss had twice booted him off. The question before the voters, Orgill said, was:

> Who is the best man for mayor? Who, as mayor, can work most effectively and most harmoniously with the four commissioners elected by you?
> Who is the most likely to bring stability to our city government?

25. Eugene Newsom, "Opinion Analysis: Memphis, Tenn.," Orgill Papers; *Commercial Appeal,* Oct. 4, 1955.

Who is pledged to prevent the formation of a political machine which could be used as a pawn in state and national elections? Who will work most effectively for expressways, traffic betterment, improved bus service, and comprehensive planning?

Who is positively committed to the building of the municipal steam plant which will guarantee the abundance of cheap electricity?[26]

While Orgill announced that council-manager government was no longer an issue in the election, Watkins Overton insisted that the reform was indeed at issue along with Orgill's other "erratic," "undemocratic," and "radical" ideas. Overton wanted the voters to know that Edmund Orgill was an advocate of:

a world-federation fad called "Atlantic Union." This movement has been condemned by the American Legion and other patriotic organizations as not being in the best interests of the United States or its people. Only last week, here in Memphis, a noted American patriot and writer said of the Atlantic Union, "it is a fetish of the millionaires and the Socialists."

Everyone in Memphis is well aware of Orgill's fanatic devotion to the City Manager form of government . . . . Imposing a city manager on Memphis is Orgill's principal goal and for years he has headed the parade for this undemocratic form of city government.

In his ambitions for world government and city manager government he shows that he is interested primarily in making radical and sweeping changes. . . . Let's not make our city Mr. Orgill's personal guinea pig.[27]

The Overton attack would surely have hurt had Orgill been a less distinguished Memphian. But to call a successful businessman "erratic" seemed unreasonable when he had the support not only of the Kefauver Democrats but also of the local Eisenhower Republicans and both the daily newspapers. Meeman's *Press-Scimitar* could be expected to support the reform candidate, but the conservative editor, Frank Ahlgren, and his *Commercial Appeal* also joined the reformers because the old leadership had let Memphis lag behind Atlanta and Dallas. The *Commercial Appeal* endorsed Orgill, stating:

There is a growing realization . . . that the time has come to put away the patch-and-mend philosophy of handling Memphis's munici-

26. *Memphis Press-Scimitar,* Oct. 24, 27, 1955; *Commercial Appeal,* Oct. 30, Nov. 3, 1955.
27. *Memphis Press-Scimitar,* Nov. 3, 1955.

pal affairs. That theme has prevailed these past few years while other cities planned and executed boldly to keep pace with the demands of a burgeoning community. . . .

Yes, we are a clean city, and a safe city. But we are also a rapidly growing city. We can't sit back and wait for state and Federal handouts year after year if we are to keep pace with challengers like Atlanta, New Orleans and Dallas. That is not the way to protect an investment or meet the needs of our people. . . .

We believe that if Edmund Orgill is elected mayor in the Nov. 10 elections he will do a lot to shake off the lethargy that closes in on city hall.[28]

An editorial endorsement by Frank Ahlgren usually reflected the thinking of the Memphis business establishment. The editor had never been accused of being an intellectual or being out of touch with his local readers. He did not even read the major journals of national opinion, nor did he join the Civic Research Committee until membership became safe and respectable. The cautious editor carefully avoided causes and crusades that might embarrass him before his tennis group or his conservative friends at the Tennessee Club. But now that the old boss was gone the business community wanted an energetic city government to bring more factories, expressways, and jobs to the city. Businessmen had no faith in Watkins Overton. The former mayor was the sort of financial conservative who, although a large downtown property owner, would not even support the Downtown Association. Merchants also recognized that Overton represented a perpetuation of the old order, which had become repugnant to so many Memphians. A vote for Overton would, for example, be a vote to perpetuate the octogenarian movie censor Lloyd T. Binford, who brought Memphis national attention for banning not only the obscene but also the films that showed blacks at a higher social level, ridiculed police, questioned patriotism, or featured an "immoral" individual such as Charlie Chaplin. Binford even prohibited the First Unitarian Church from including one of Chaplin's movies in its Sunday night film classics by explaining that the comedian was "a dirty, filthy character."[29] A

28. *Commercial Appeal,* Oct. 16, 1955; Frank Ahlgren interview, Mississippi Valley Collection.
29. Interview with Lucius E. Burch, Jr., Sanitation Strike Project, Mississippi

good many Memphians felt Binford's tyranny to be an intolerable restraint on individual freedom and bad publicity that made Memphis a laughingstock of the nation. Even businessmen could agree with literary intellectuals that the old leadership had kept Memphis out of step with other American cities.

Black voters also rejected Watkins Overton as a symbol of the old order. Overton had opposed the election of a Negro to the school board. Edmund Orgill had supported Dr. Walker's candidacy and had worked with him and other black leaders in the Kefauver campaigns, fund drives for the Collins Chapel Hospital, and the Civic Research Committee. Black leadership rallied to Orgill's support. Ministers who typically avoided politics, such as the greatly respected Reverend S. A. Owen, now issued an endorsement: "Mr. Edmund Orgill has been doing big, unselfish things in and for Memphis for many years and he has not done them with an eye single to political preferences. The matter of office has not come into consideration. It is my impression that he is a successful businessman with a big heart and a generous spirit. He is a humanitarian and a Christian gentleman."[30]

Blacks conducted their own energetic campaign and voter registration effort. The two insurance executives who monopolized black political leadership, J. E. Walker and Lieutenant George W. Lee, had decided to enter a shouting Baptist minister, Reverend Roy Love, in the campaign for a seat on the Memphis Board of Education and thereby actively involve the black clergy in both the campaign and the voter registration. The politicians reckoned that 90 percent of the city's black adults held membership in at least one of the 250 local churches, so that the clergy must hold the keys to the unregistered voters. They convened a small meeting of the two dozen community leaders to endorse popular Reverend Love, then they arranged the largest local leadership assembly in a quarter of a century. Two hundred ministers and secular leaders came together at the Pentecostal Temple Church of God in Christ. Honoring the

---

Valley Collection, Brister Library, Memphis State Univ.; Ahlgren interview; *Memphis Press-Scimitar,* Feb. 19, April 9, 24, 1954, Feb. 7, 1955.

30. S. A. Owen to Orgill Campaign for Mayor, Nov. 3, 1955, CRC Papers; *Tri-State Defender,* Oct. 22, Nov. 2, 12, 19, 1955.

request of the politicians, churchmen from all the black denominations put aside their rivalries and organized the Ministers and Citizens League. They approved a $2,000 registration budget, hired
three full-time secretaries, and pledged their automobiles and their
churches to the work of doubling the number of registered black
voters. Black pastors preached citizenship, conducted mass meetings, and drove unregistered parishioners to the court house, adding
5,000 names to the registration lists and raising the registered black
vote to 39,000. The black vote was committed to both Reverend
Love and Edmund Orgill. Even Watkins Overton's political advisers were reporting that blacks would cast more than 75 percent of
their ballots for Edmund Orgill.[31]

Orgill's friends in the Civic Research Committee were no longer
political amateurs, and this time they conducted a professional campaign. With the experience and the campaign files from Kefauver's
two past victories, they conducted intensive work in wards and precincts. In addition, they were joined by those Eisenhower Republicans who were members of the Civic Research Committee and who
now contributed their Republican political files and firm support
for Edmund Orgill. Mrs. Gwen Awsumb, an energetic Republican
housewife, joined liberal Frances Coe as co-chairman of Orgill's
precinct work. Their volunteer workers were active in all but six of
the city's 129 precincts. Orgill benefited from inspired television
programs and the support of the business establishment, labor, and
blacks. And so, on election day, the reform candidate won with 61
percent of the vote.[32]

After decades of machine rule, independent business and professional leaders now rejoiced: "We were delighted. This election has
restored the faith of citizens in themselves and in democratic pro-
cesses." "The result of yesterday's election is evidence that you can

31. Lloyd T. Binford to Watkins Overton, Nov. 4, 1955; Box 7, Overton Papers;
Tucker, *Black Pastors and Leaders,* 108–11; *Memphis Press-Scimitar,* Aug. 17,
1955; *Memphis World,* Aug. 19, 1955; *Tri-State Defender,* Sept. 10, 1955; interview
with Roy Love, Feb. 4, 1970.
32. Frances Coe interview, Mississippi Valley Collection; *Memphis Press-
Scimitar,* Nov. 11, 1955. Only half of the registered black voters showed up at the
polls, and school board candidate Roy Love, even with some white support, received
20,082 votes, or 5,000 fewer than he needed to win one of the four at-large seats.

trust the judgment of the people when given free elections." Memphis would now be led by an executive educated by municipal experts and devoted to good government. "With your qualities of leadership, foresight and courage," a businessman wrote, "I'm sure a new era of sound, planned progress and growth is in store for this great metropolis." Even intellectuals were delighted, and a professor at local Southwestern University summed up his expectations: "I can foresee a rebirth of civic consciousness," John Osman said, "my mind goes back to my beloved Florence, Italy. It was Lorenzo de Medici—a businessman-banker and textile manufacturer—who led the city to her highest moment in the history of western civilization. Not only was Lorenzo de Medici a businessman, but he was a student of politics, economics and human affairs. He gathered around him the intellectual leadership of the age. The result—the flowering of Florence that we describe as the Renaissance."[33]

33. Peyton N. Rhodes to Orgill, Nov. 11, 1955; Thurston Roach to Orgill, Nov. 11, 1955; Charles T. Wheat to Orgill, Nov. 11, 1955; John Osman to Orgill, Nov. 14, 1955, Orgill Papers.

5.

The Orgill Administration

Urban renewal became a revival gospel shared by the local elite and voiced in testimonial meetings such as the Forward Memphis dinner that followed the local elections of 1955. At the beginning of the civic banquet, which was sponsored by the local chamber of commerce, Arthur B. Van Buskirk, a Pennsylvania corporation attorney, told 600 Memphians how dirty and decayed Pittsburgh had experienced an amazing revitalization through cooperative efforts of business, labor, and government. Pittsburgh would later discover that rebuilding its central business district brought no solution for the problems of unemployment, housing, and race, but in the fifties Buskirk and the urban experts still assumed downtowns were the driving force of metropolitan prosperity and that the new Pittsburgh Golden Triangle would create a general wellbeing and correct other metropolitan problems. After the story of Pittsburgh's presumed success with urban renewal, representatives from each of fifty-two Memphis civic clubs delivered one-minute testimonials, pledging their cooperation in building a great metropolitan Memphis. The civic enthusiasm and virtual unanimity of opinion on that evening of November 29, 1955 persuaded Edmund Orgill that he had indeed chosen "a grand time" to be mayor.[1]

1. *Memphis Press-Scimitar,* Nov. 21, 30, 1955; *Commercial Appeal,* Nov. 27, 30, 1955.

Even the remnants of the Crump machine seemed to join in the general enthusiasm for progressive urban government. Acting mayor Walter Chandler saved Orgill the embarrassment of having to fire Mrs. Will Fowler and the other twenty-seven women on the City Beautiful Commission. It had outlived its usefulness and now threatened to spend $130,000 a year on little more than teas and luncheons. Chandler notified the women that their jobs would terminate December 31. This protected the new mayor from political trouble and also provided the money necessary for hiring a competent planning commission.[2]

Consolidation of the separate and inadequate city and county planning agencies was Orgill's most urgent goal. If Memphis were destined to annex much of Shelby County, any reasonable man could see the wisdom of planning and extending sewers, roads, and zoning regulations beyond the present city limits. Even the Shelby County commissioners agreed with Orgill that the two existing planning commissions should be combined and provided with a trained professional staff. David N. Harsh, chairman of the County Commission after the death of E. W. Hale, was an attorney and real estate developer who certainly believed and profited from urban growth. He agreed: "planning must be done so the city can grow without overcrowding." So Orgill was able to secure an agreement between city and county government, before he took office, to create a single Memphis–Shelby County Planning Commission with a professional staff.[3]

Mayor Orgill rushed through an almost continuous round of meetings and conferences. He backed the reforms he had learned from seven years of membership in the National Municipal League and the Civic Research Committee. If consolidation of two planning commissions was efficient and progressive, then so would be the union of the two tax assessors' offices and the two public school

2. *Commercial Appeal,* Dec. 11, 1955. Mayor Chandler took a personal delight in firing Mrs. Fowler, who had always communicated directly with Mr. Crump and ignored both the mayor and the other city commissioners. Interview with Edmund Orgill, Aug. 12, 1973.

3. *Commercial Appeal,* Jan. 16, 22, 31, 1956; *Memphis Press-Scimitar,* Dec. 20, 31, 1955.

systems. A single metropolitan government was the mayor's goal for Shelby County. While working for unification and efficiency, Orgill also sought to implement Harland Bartholomew's *Comprehensive Plan: Memphis, Tennessee,* the recently completed guide for the city to follow over the next quarter of a century. Half the study's hundred pages were devoted to consequences of the automobile, which had tripled in numbers over the last decade, requiring blueprints of new streets, expressways, and parking for solving traffic congestion. Major streets—Poplar, Lamar, and Union—were to be expanded from four to six traffic lanes. New schools, parks, and open spaces were planned for an urban area that would grow to 800,000 by 1980. The study called for a civic center of new public buildings clustered together on the fringe of downtown Memphis to enhance the appearance of the central business district and to strengthen the pride of Memphis citizens. The entire cost of streets, parks, public buildings, urban renewals, and sewers was estimated at $200 million, enough to send cold shivers through the spines of older Crump politicians. With federal aid, an annual seven million dollar bond issue, and a tax increase, the city could easily afford the municipal improvements. Orgill pushed ahead with the plans but the old city and county politicians began a stubborn resistance.[4]

Opposition should have been no surprise. The Orgill crowd had gambled all on the mayor's race, refusing to endorse a slate of commissioners pledged to support the Civic Research program. Not one of the four commissioners elected in 1955 owed any allegiance to Edmund Orgill. Three had been machine politicians: Claude A. Armour and John T. Dwyer had worked their way up through Crump's police department and had then been promoted to the commission; Stanley Dillard had worked twenty-four years for Crump's park commission before he was fired for supporting Overton. Even the fourth commissioner, Henry Loeb III, should not have been considered favorable to Orgill. The young laundry executive was no team player. He had once worked for Crump; he won the presidency of the local American Legion in 1952 with the old

4. Harlan Bartholomew and Associates, *Comprehensive Plan: Memphis, Tenn.* (St. Louis: HBA, 1955); *Commercial Appeal,* Jan. 3, 15, March 11, April 29, 1956.

man's blessings. But he turned, after Crump died, to attack the remnants of the machine with a gusto which endeared him to many of the same independents who supported Orgill. He never became a member of Orgill's group, however. He refused ever to join the Civic Research Committee or Federal Union. Young Loeb seemed an ambitious opportunist willing to move any way the political breeze blew. None of the four commissioners was certain to follow Orgill's leadership.

Shelby County politicians were even less inclined to embrace Orgill's ideas. The chairman of the county commission, David N. Harsh, was known for his abrasive personality. The conservative and outspoken Harsh had no intention of permitting Orgill a free hand in local government. But even a more reasonable gentleman such as County Commissioner Rudolph Jones could find much to resist in Mayor Orgill. Jones had a patrician family background, an engineering degree from Washington and Lee University, and the idealism of a hero worshipper who memorized Woodrow Wilson's guiding maxims: "Live by enthusiasm. Don't be driven by necessity. If you fail, make failure a stepping stone." Even though the Hale-Crump machine had elected Jones to office in 1946 he was a civil engineer and no politician. As county commissioner responsible for roads, bridges, and the Shelby County Penal Farm, he removed leg chains from the prisoners, taught them concrete construction, and replaced the county's 1,200 wooden bridges. Even a modest, diligent, and energetic public servant such as Jones found Mayor Orgill overbearing and undiplomatic in his eagerness fully to consolidate city and county government. So Jones joined his fellow county commissioners in resisting the reforms of Edmund Orgill.[5]

Public policy toward black Memphians became an issue that separated Orgill from the other politicians. Initially, the question was whether blacks could use a municipal golf course for the tournament of the Central States Golf Association. The former mayor Tobey had promised blacks the use of a white municipal golf course (there were no eighteen-hole golf courses for blacks in Memphis), but increased white hostility towards blacks emerged because the

5. Interview with Rudolph Jones, March 18, 1974.

U.S. Supreme Court declared segregation of public golf courses unconstitutional. In November 1955, the Memphis NAACP asked the city to respect the recent court decisions, open its parks to blacks, and integrate the local public schools as well. The White Citizens Council, organized to express local white opposition to black requests, and city commissioners grew reluctant to carry out Tobey's promise. With support from the *Memphis Press-Scimitar,* Orgill wisely decided to hold a public hearing and ask his friends to come and speak for tolerance and reason. Reverend Marshall Wingfield, Reverend Paul Tudor Jones, and attorney George Grider were there to answer the heated voices of the White Citizens Council, the Pro-Southerners, and We, The People. When white segregationists predicted violence if approval were given for the tournament, Orgill dramatically asked, "Would anyone in this room be a party to violence and bloodshed? If so, stand up." No one stood up. After four hours of unreasonable rhetoric by the segregationists and sensible logic by Orgill's friends, the commissioners followed Orgill back to his office and voted unanimously to support former mayor Tobey's commitment and let blacks use a white golf course. Thus began a tolerant racial policy for the Orgill administration.[6]

Orgill had managed to hold his commission together during the golf course controversy, but he lost them all when he attempted to make a black appointment. Orgill sympathized with black aspirations for equality because he had come to know middle-class leaders through his interracial civic and political work. Being personally fair and just, he had to admit that these blacks were as well educated and as reasonable as whites. He had wanted to appoint Dr. J.E. Walker to the board of John Gaston Hospital because he believed that such an appointment was the easiest way to bring blacks into local government. The other commissioners had absolutely refused. After the golf course controversy, Orgill again pushed Walker's nomination. This time he went directly to the public by announcing in a television interview that a Negro should be appointed to the hospital board because blacks represented 40 percent of the city

6. Interview with Orgill, July 14, 1973; *Commercial Appeal,* Nov. 30, 1955, Feb. 15, 1956; *Memphis Press-Scimitar,* Jan. 14, Feb. 13-15, 1956.

population and 85 percent of the patients in John Gaston Hospital. Appointing a black businessman would help blacks consider themselves a part of the government, Orgill explained, and they would then feel more obligated to help support city law. Orgill's recommendation of a black drew denunciation from the four other commissioners even before the general public had an opportunity to respond. Many indignant white Memphians made midnight telephone calls to the mayor's home and turned in false fire alarms for his address at 1490 Linden. He abandoned his black nomination.[7]

When a federal district court ruled in early June 1956 that bus segregation in Montgomery, Alabama was unconstitutional, black Memphians promptly filed suit charging local discrimination. Mayor Orgill recommended to his fellow commissioners that blacks be permitted to sit anywhere they pleased. The other commissioners wanted to defend Memphis segregation in the courts for political reasons, but they promised Orgill that they would uphold whatever decision the Supreme Court delivered in a Memphis case. Delay thus became the Memphis policy. Orgill did use the court delay to work for future success of desegregation by urging editor Frank Ahlgren to publicize the peaceful results of bus integration in other Southern cities: Edward Meeman, of course, had always spoken for moderation and never needed a sermon from the mayor. Orgill immediately sought improved treatment of blacks by white bus drivers, urging the head of the privately owned Memphis Street Railway Company to insist on politeness. He wrote directly to the labor leader of the drivers, W. C. "Switchbar" Johnson, to suggest that the union ought to do all in its power to avoid a Montgomery-style bus boycott that would cost many bus drivers their jobs and disturb the tranquillity of the city. "I think I know how you feel about this matter," Mayor Orgill wrote, "and the purpose of this letter is simply to tell you privately that I hope that you will use every bit of influence you have to encourage pleasantness and politeness to all riders, including Negroes."[8]

As Mayor Orgill pursued racial harmony, he read the black weekly

7. Interview with Orgill, July 14, 1973; *Commercial Appeal,* Feb. 28, 29, 1956.
8. Orgill to W. C. "Switchbar" Johnson, March 3, 1956, Orgill Papers; *Commercial Appeal,* June 6, 1956; interview with Orgill, July 14, 1973; although O. Z. Evers

Tri-State Defender. He reported cases of police brutality to Commissioner Claude Armour and also requested that Frank Ahlgren expose cases of police prejudice in the *Commercial Appeal.* He even took a few moderate steps to secure white acceptance of desegregation rulings by the Supreme Court. During speaking engagements before civic clubs, Orgill used the opportunity to mention the school desegregation decisions and suggest that "integration would not be the end of the world" for Memphis, that the neighborhood school system would permit only token integration, and that the best families now sent their children off for an education at Vassar and Harvard, which were integrated. When pressed for his personal opinion in April 1957, Orgill did not admit to being an integrationist ("I have never advocated or desired integration . . . ," he would say). He preferred to emphasize that the important issues were keeping the peace, upholding the law, and remembering that all men were God's children. Certainly Orgill's efforts at race relations were enough to win a 1956 Merit Award from the *Tri-State Defender* and to avoid any major black confrontation during his administration.[9]

The moderate mayor had loyal support from fellow reformers who quickly organized the Greater Memphis Race Relations Committee for interracial discussions designed to preserve interracial good will, avoid violence, and delay desegregation. The committee was initially led by attorney George Grider, Orgill's campaign manager, who told influential white Memphians, "The Negroes have the law on their side. If they bring this matter into court they'll win." Much of the Memphis establishment, including staunch segregationists, was recruited into the GMRRC. The local black establishment went along with the committee. They too were alarmed by growing extremist sentiment among whites and shared a faith in the good intentions of Orgill and his friends. The black president of local LeMoyne College, Dr. Hollis Price, said, "I suspect most Negroes here are quite content with a gradual approach to integration."

---

filed his suit in 1956, local buses would remain segregated until after the local sit-ins of 1960.

9. Orgill to Claude Armour, May 23, 1957; Orgill to Mrs. G. A. Coors, May 6, 1958, Orgill Papers; *Tri-State Defender,* Dec. 1, 1956; *Memphis Press-Scimitar,* April 3, 1957.

Dr. Price conceded that he was willing to wait five to ten years for integration. Lieutenant George Lee, the major black political leader, would not be pinned down to a time table but agreed, "we'll play along with the committee as long as we feel it will do something."[10]

Taxes, rather than race, actually became the most divisive issue within the Orgill administration. The price of rapid city redevelopment was plainly an increase in the property tax, the major revenue producer for local government. But three commissioners—Claude Armour, John T. Dwyer, and Stanley Dillard—had learned their politics in the Crump organization. They knew low taxes were the best means of securing reelection and refused to raise Mr. Crump's tax rate even though more than half the increased revenue would go to the public schools. The newspapers and the chamber of commerce favored the tax increase, but the three commissioners voted it down in March, 1956. Orgill was never able to raise the tax rate at all. Crump's officials did increase city revenues by having the tax assessor reappraise property and raise its assessed value, thus collecting more taxes while boasting that they had kept the old tax rate of $1.80.[11]

During the tax controversy, members of the old Crump machine organized as the Citizens for Progress (CP), dedicated to the conservative goals of the existing tax rate, the commission form of city government, and the segregation system. The idea of racial integration aroused enormous anger in 1956 as the white South grew alarmed over threatening integration of the public schools. At the organizing session of Citizens for Progress, the main speaker, Representative Cliff Davis, attacked the Supreme Court and Senator Estes Kefauver. The senator had not only refused to sign the Southern Manifesto against the school desegregation decision but also campaigned for the Democratic presidential nomination by endorsing civil rights for black Americans. The attack on Senator Kefauver was generally considered to be directed as well at Mayor Orgill, who shared Kefauver's liberalism. The misnamed Citizens for Prog-

10. *Commercial Appeal,* Feb. 23, 28, March 2, 1956; *Tri-State Defender,* March 25, 31, 1956; *Memphis Press-Scimitar,* March 26, 27, 1956.
11. *Commercial Appeal,* March 5, 8, 11, 14, 1956; interview with Orgill, Aug. 12, 1973.

ress certainly included all of Orgill's political enemies—every county officeholder and Claude Armour, John T. Dwyer, and Stanley Dillard from the city commission. When the conservative group ran their state legislative ticket for the 1956 elections, they campaigned under the segregationist slogan—"Keep Memphis and Shelby County Down in Dixie"—clearly exploiting the race issue.[12]

Orgill's friends—3,500 strong—rallied together for an enormous barbecue at the Thomas L. Robinson farm. They formed their own political action group, one that Edward Meeman had long been advocating, a citizens' association modeled after those of Cincinnati, Kansas City, and Philadelphia. Leaders of the nonpartisan Civic Research Committee became officers of the new Good Local Government League, released from CRC charter restraints and free to write a political platform, interview politicians, and endorse a slate of candidates for the state legislature.[13] These state positions were very important to local government because Memphis, not yet legally a city with home rule, was forced to go through the state legislature for most reforms of city government.

Lucius Burch had been the sparkplug for the new citizens' association. He sent National Municipal League booklets on organizing and winning civic campaigns to twenty key members of the Civic Research Committee and then called them together to plan a citizens' league. Before the first public meeting in the Hotel Chisca, Edward Meeman editorially announced that he would gladly attend in order to see "what I've wanted to see ever since I came to Memphis in 1931."

> I'll see citizens form an organization to make the choosing and support of local government their own business rather than the business of politicians.
> For I believe this is the basic need of every community—the foundation on which all other civic life should be built.
> It is the basic need of our free way of life—for only when we are assured democratic, clean, efficient government in our cities and counties can we be sure we will have the kind of state and national politics which

12. *Commercial Appeal,* March 23, April 14, July 6, 1956; Orgill to Clifford Davis, April 13, 1956, Orgill Papers.
13. *Commercial Appeal,* May 27, June 9, 11, 27, July 14, 1956; Lucius E. Burch, Jr. to Friends, April 11, 1956, Orgill Papers.

is also an expression of responsible, dedicated citizens rather than of prejudices, passions and self-interest.[14]

Two hundred and seventy-five Memphians turned out to organize the Good Local Government League (GLGL). The group was politically bipartisan since local reformers now controlled the party machinery of both Shelby County parties. The Republican chairman, Walker Wellford, Jr., was there to describe the organization as one of the finest things ever to happen in the community. Leaders of organized labor who had been in the old CIO struggles—W. A. "Red" Copeland and George "Rip" Clark—were there to work against the Citizens for Progress. In recognition of labor's importance, the president of the local CIO council, W. H. Crawford, was made first vice-president of GLGL. Blacks held no offices or directorships in the GLGL, but they were members. Dr. J. E. Walker and forty other blacks attended the Hotel Chisca meeting, one of the first desegregated events in local downtown hotels, and Reverend S. A. Owen was made chairman of the GLGL committee to interview Republicans about their attitude towards the goals of home rule, school consolidation, exclusion of local public employees from political work, and university status for Memphis State College.[15]

Photographs of the integrated meetings of the Good Local Government League provided the opposition with evidence to support the charge that the Orgill group approved of integration. At Citizens for Progress rallies, photographs were held high to show that blacks and whites were really meeting together and that the league candidates were indeed the race-mixing ticket. To save Memphis from this "group of star-gazers and pseudo-intellectuals and screwballs," Memphians were urged to vote for the ticket supported by Citizens for Progress.[16]

None of the candidates endorsed by the GLGL actually advocated integration. And George Grider, chairman of the reform organization, sought to persuade the voters that the Citizens for Progress were only attempting to create hysteria by interjecting racial ques-

14. *Memphis Press-Scimitar,* June 20, 1956; Burch to Friends, April 11, 1956, Orgill Papers.
15. *Commercial Appeal,* June 9, 22, 1956.
16. *Ibid.,* July 26, Aug. 5, 1956.

tions into the campaign. A CP candidate for the senate, Tom Mitchell, retorted, "George Grider of the 'gluck glucks' was in the submarine service—I think he must have stayed underwater too long." It was true that Grider had been a submarine commander and had not publicly admitted that he was an integrationist. After growing up on an Arkansas plantation, Grider attended Annapolis, and earned highest war honors as commander of the *Flasher,* which sank more enemy tonnage than any other U.S. submarine during World War II. When heart trouble forced him out of the navy in 1947 he earned a law degree at the University of Virginia and came home to Memphis as an attorney in 1950. Grider quickly moved into the reformer circle and his competitive enthusiasm soon made him a member of Lucius Burch's law firm, campaign manager for Orgill, and temporary chairman of the Greater Memphis Race Relations Committee.[17]

When voters went to the polls in August they decisively rejected the legislative candidates endorsed by George Grider and the GLGL, apparently preferring conservative candidates pledged to segregation and low taxes rather than moderate and progressive local government. Orgill and his friends had lost in their effort to influence the election of Shelby County's state representatives.[18]

Mayor Orgill frequently seemed more like a college professor than a politician when he opposed the majority opinion on race, taxes, and the commission form of government. He not only repeatedly criticized the commission form but also invited to Memphis the annual convention of the National Municipal League, which offered civics lessons in the wisdom of city manager government, urban planning, and city-county consolidation. To expose the public to the experts, Orgill arranged a televised panel discussion among officials of the league in addition to the regular public sessions held in the Peabody Hotel. He insisted that not only academic experts but also businessmen be included in the program. In particular, Orgill persuaded a banker from Dallas, where the council-manager form of government had prospered, to speak on "The Businessman in Local Politics." "What we want you to do," Orgill told R.L.

17. *Memphis Press-Scimitar,* June 28, July 16, 18, 1956.
18. *Commercial Appeal,* June 27, July 26, Aug. 5, 1956.

Thornton, "is to show how the leading businessmen of Dallas have taken an interest in their local government and . . . try to let our businessmen know that it is not going to 'hurt their business,' to stick their necks out and become active in local governmental affairs."[19] Naturally, Orgill's efforts to build an active citizens' reform movement of businessmen created resentment among the old practical politicians—the city commissioners who feared good government as a threat to their political future.

The bitter division between Orgill and the three commissioners of the Citizens for Progress led to many petty insults (Orgill's appointments were blocked and his authority over the city park system was trimmed), producing a general belief that city hall had been so wracked by dissension that all cooperation had ceased.[20] But despite the political divisiveness, the Orgill years produced many urban improvements that were approved by the commission and then paid for with borrowed money from the bond markets. Biggest of all was the $163 million electric generating plant. The conservative Republican national administration refused to support the efforts of the Tennessee Valley Authority to build a new generating plant to meet the growing electrical needs of Memphis; it preferred to support private power and the Dixon-Yates contract for West Memphis. Mayor Frank Tobey had vowed Memphis would never buy from Dixon-Yates, and his commission voted on June 23, 1955 to build a municipal power plant. Cheap public power was very popular in Memphis, and Thomas H. Allen of the Memphis Light, Gas, and Water Division had urged that if TVA could not supply enough power, then the city should build its own plant. On becoming mayor, Edmund Orgill carried out the decision to build by issuing the bonds and constructing the world's largest municipally owned power system, the Allen Steam Plant.[21]

19. *Ibid.,* May 20, 22, 1956; Orgill to R. L. Thornton, July 30, 1956, Orgill Papers; Burch to Alfred Willoughby, Nov. 22, 1955; Allen H. Seed to Charles Pool, Feb. 29, 1956, Civic Research Committee Papers.

20. *Commercial Appeal,* Oct. 3, 5, 1956; *Memphis Press-Scimitar,* March 20, 1957.

21. The national controversy has been explained by Aaron Wildavsky, *Dixon-Yates: A Study in Power Politics* (New Haven: Yale Univ. Press, 1962); the local controversy in which the Memphis Chamber of Commerce supported Dixon-Yates

Annexation of Frayser also moved forward during Orgill's first months in office. A cost study reported in March 1956 that to annex the poorly developed blue-collar community would cost an initial two million dollars for sewers, school buildings, streets, and fire stations, and that more than a million a year would be spent providing standard city services. Property taxes from Frayser would bring in only half a million dollars. Annexation would be expensive for Memphis. The four commissioners delayed bringing the community in until January 1, 1958. Mayor Orgill failed to persuade his commission to annex other areas. He had hoped to annex everything south of Memphis to the Mississippi state line, including the white middle-class community of Whitehaven. Its 30,000 inhabitants would help boost Memphis above its current ranking as the twenty-sixth largest city in America. Despite the mayor's emphasis on the importance of annexation in time for the 1960 census, fear of creating new expenses prevented the other commissioners from approving further annexation, and the city became only the twenty-second largest.[22]

Expressway construction finally began during the Orgill administration as part of the national interstate system to be paid for by state and federal funds. The Bartholomew plan called for one freeway circling the city and another cutting east and west through Memphis. The outer route aroused a minimum of objections. But the internal route, which the downtown merchants wanted most, created much protest that focused on the plans to bulldoze twenty-four acres of virgin woodland in Overton Park, Memphis's finest municipal park. With his faith in experts, Mayor Orgill backed the

---

can only be understood by reading the files of Mayor Frank Tobey (1954) in the Memphis City Archives; an overview of public power in Memphis can be found in *Commercial Appeal,* Feb. 24–25, 1961, June 7, 1964; Memphis proved unable to produce electricity as cheaply as TVA, and Edmund Orgill pressured the reluctant, bureaucratic MLGW to lease the steam plant to TVA in 1963 and purchase electricity again from TVA.

22. Will Fowler et al. to Orgill, March 6, 1956; Henry Loeb to Orgill, May 17, 1956; Orgill to Claude Armour, July 29, 1957; Orgill to Commissioners, Sept. 13, 1958, Oct. 19, 1959, Orgill Papers; for a sociological study of Whitehaven, see Roger Alan Bates, "The Relationship between Socio-Economic Status and Religious Behavior in a Mid-South Suburb" (M.A. thesis, Memphis State Univ., 1968).

Bartholomew engineers who had selected the route. He held public meetings in which he unsuccessfully sought to explain the logic to property owners from the Overton Park neighborhood. Vocal opposition however, was not responsible for delaying construction of the internal expressway. The state highway commissioner simply decided to begin first on the southern half of the circumferential interstate, and construction work started there in 1958.[23]

Urban renewal also began with the Orgill administration. When the 1949 Federal Housing Act made postwar slum clearance possible, the Crump administration refused to support the plans advanced by the Memphis Housing Authority. This was due largely to opposition from realtors and home builders, who proposed their own plan for a war on slums. The city did adopt a stricter housing code and sent out inspectors who went from block to block. Outside toilets and water supplies were condemned, and rehabilitation or destruction of substandard houses was required. Despite a great deal of talk about the city and the cooperative slum clearance program undertaken by local home builders, work did not get underway until 1955, when Memphis clearly needed federal aid in eliminating local slums.[24]

Mayor Orgill believed in both slum clearance and public housing. The five local public housing developments built just before the Second World War had been successful operations in which the residents took considerable pride and which they kept clean and neat. The Memphis Housing Authority, which administered the public housing, publicized its cleaner, healthier atmosphere for 4,491 families, arguing that it encouraged respect for the law and even that the experience of improved housing elevated the tastes of its residents, motivating them to seek even better private housing. In five years, 6,494 families had moved from public housing, and of these fami-

23. Bartholomew, *Comprehensive Plan: Memphis, Tenn.,* 37, plate 16; M. A. Hinds to Jack Carley, April 25, 1957, Hinds Papers, Mississippi Valley Collection; *Commercial Appeal,* May 26, Sept. 22, 1957; *Memphis Press-Scimitar,* May 29, Sept. 18, 1957, June 6, Sept. 11, 1958.

24. *Memphis Press-Scimitar,* Dec. 5, 1951, July 15, 1953, Feb. 2, 9, April 4, 1955; Walter M. Simmons to Orgill, June 12, 1956, Orgill Papers; the Memphis cooperative plan won a Slum Clearance Award in 1957 from *Look* magazine and improved more housing than did the federal program.

lies, one out of seven had bought a house. The housing authority's *Annual Report* for 1956 used as an example the success story of Elvis Presley, a local boy who had learned the sound of black blues and become a millionaire:

> A typical example of this rapid turnover is the case of Mr. and Mrs. Vernon Presley and their now-famous son, Elvis.
>
> Elvis and his parents were sharing one room in a boarding house at 572 Poplar in 1949. All three of them slept in one room and shared a cold bath down the hall with several other boarders.
>
> Then they moved into Lauderdale Courts—and a comfortable, attractive, private, two-bedroom apartment.
>
> Elvis was 15 then and worked summers as an usher in Loew's Theatre. In the winter, he continued at Humes High School. The next summer, Elvis shared a more profitable $27-a-week job with Precision Tool Co. Meanwhile, his father was doing better financially, too.
>
> By 1953, after four years in public housing and a long time before Elvis began singing professionally, the Presleys had reached the maximum ceiling rent of $56.40 and could stay in public housing no longer.
>
> They bought their own home at Kimball and Getwell and moved in immediately.[25]

The Memphis Housing Authority exaggerated in calling the Presleys "typical." The average family would have been black because two-thirds of the participants in the Memphis program had always been black. The paternalistic Crump organization had recognized the greater housing needs of black Memphians, three-fourths of whom lived in substandard housing in the thirties, and it took pride in the segregated housing projects for blacks. By the time Orgill became mayor, housing had improved until only a third of black Memphians remained in dilapidated housing. But with an average family income of $1,348—one-third of the white income—the expanding black population obtained no more than 10 percent of the new privately built housing, and blacks were forced to seek housing in older all-white areas, arousing much racial hostility in whites. To reduce racial friction and to meet the black need for low-cost housing, the Memphis Housing Authority during Orgill's administration constructed 600 additional apartments for blacks (and none for

25. Memphis Housing Authority, *1956 Annual Report*; Jerry Hopkins, *Elvis: A Biography* (New York: Simon and Schuster, 1971), 1–73.

whites) in the Joseph A. Fowler Homes and the Henry E. Oates Manor.[26]

Orgill would have pushed for more slum clearance and public housing if money had been available. In fact, he told the National Housing Conference that the federal government should double its contribution, giving four dollars for every city dollar spent to clear slums.[27] With limited resources, the Orgill administration could do no more than successfully push the Railroad Avenue and the Jackson Avenue Projects, the first urban renewal projects in Memphis, and begin three more developments—Riverview, the medical center, and the civic center—to enhance the downtown area.

The river bluff below downtown Memphis was a decaying area of warehouses and railroad yards that thoughtful Memphians believed should be the showplace of the city. It featured high-rise luxury apartments in a park setting that overlooked the bend in the Mississippi River. Planning for the 135-acre Riverview Project began in 1956 with great enthusiasm. Bulldozing the site followed after Orgill left office, but then the cautious Memphis supporters withdrew financial backing from the project, which had the approval of the planners, the architects, and the artists. "This bluff on the bend of the river could be the most beautiful thing outside of Rio," novelist Shelby Foote said almost two decades later. "Really. There is no more magnificent place to build a city than Memphis. It would take a billion dollars to develop the bluff but it could be done. Then, you'd have a bustling, going, big taxpaying city instead of a dying river town."[28]

Memphis never deserved to be described as a dying river town—the city suburbs were expanding rapidly—but the riverfront was badly decayed, and the general poverty of the population so frightened timid private capital that no one would purchase the river sites for urban renewal. With the income of the average Memphis family

26. James E. Kerwin to Orgill, April 2, 1956, J. A. McDaniel to Orgill, Jan. 18, 1957, Orgill Papers; *Benefits and Opportunities for Colored Citizens of Memphis* (Memphis: 1945), 22–23; Louis Gambill, *Memphis Civic Progress* (Memphis: City of Memphis, 1945), 67–69.

27. Orgill, "Manuscript Speech to National Housing Conference," June 23, 1958, Orgill Papers.

28. *Commercial Appeal,* Sept. 27, 1956, Sept. 10, 1957, April 1, 4, 1973.

one-fourth less than the average in Atlanta or Dallas, and with only 10 percent of Memphis families earning more than $10,000 in 1959, cautious bankers were unwilling to invest in luxury development of the riverfront. When the choice restaurant location was advertised for sale, only the First Unitarian Church entered a bid. The congregation used the riverfront property to build a church and not a restaurant.[29]

It seemed that only the urban renewal projects constructed with public money would be outstanding successes in Memphis. The medical center and the civic center, both planned under Orgill and later constructed with public funds, would be points of great civic pride. Urban renewal tore out slum property surrounding a cluster of hospitals and the University of Tennessee Medical Colleges to create an expanded 138-acre medical complex in the central city, providing patient care, medical education, and health research. The medical center employed more than 27,000 persons by 1970, spent more than a quarter of a billion dollars annually, and was regarded by Memphians as one of the largest and finest health centers in the nation.[30]

Edmund Orgill worked toward a civic center even before he took office as mayor. The Bartholomew plan had called for an impressive cluster of public buildings to anchor the northern edge of the central business district, and even before his inauguration Orgill was writing Senators Kefauver and Gore to ask for help in securing a new federal office building. Orgill appealed to Governor Frank Clement for a state office building. A new city hall and a county building were also to be included in the center. Once beyond the time-consuming process of securing commitments to construct the buildings, the civic center plans moved more rapidly. The League of Memphis Architects designed the center on a nonprofit basis in 1959, and actual construction was completed during the next decade.[31]

29. *Ibid.,* April 2, 1973.
30. Clayton Braddock, "Memphis Medical Center," *Memphis* 1 (July 1970), 38–43.
31. Interview with Orgill, July 14, 1973; Orgill to Walter Chandler, Dec. 2, 1955; Orgill to Frank Clement, Jan. 6, 1956, Orgill Papers; League of Architects, *Memphis Civic Center* (Memphis: League, 1959).

The achievements of the Orgill administration were accompanied by much political bickering and delay, which distressed the mayor and made him responsive to Estes Kefauver's repeated requests that he run for governor in 1958. A state-wide movement for Orgill launched by Kefauver supporters and backed by Orgill's Memphis friends persuaded the mayor of a genuine draft. But the year following integration in Little Rock schools was not a time when a Southern moderate could win by urging compliance with law and court orders. Ed Meeman's *Press-Scimitar* enthusiastically advocated Orgill's candidacy, but the *Commercial Appeal* took a bitter stand against federally forced integration and was supporting the most rabid of the segregationists, Andrew T. Taylor. The opposition of the *Commercial Appeal* appears to have been entirely a matter of Scripps-Howard profits. While editor Frank Ahlgren privately worked with Meeman and Orgill for moderation, his newspaper publicly played to the segregationists. Orgill lost the support of his own Shelby County over the integration issue on election day and yet came within 9,000 votes of winning the governor's race.[32]

After the gubernatorial defeat, Orgill ran for reelection as mayor. He hoped to complete his capital improvements program—the civic center, expressway construction, and the airport expansion. New programs also needed to be undertaken, such as consolidation of the many rail lines which cluttered the city, construction of a new sports stadium and coliseum at the fairgrounds, and especially unification of city and county governments. Orgill had long been convinced by planners and the National Municipal League that metropolitan areas could be effectively and economically administered only by ending the multiplicity of governmental units. The Memphis-Shelby County squabble over school money emerged as persuasive evidence of the friction and chaos created by the old system of competing units of government. When Shelby County received its share of the state public school money, the county commissioners should

32. Estes Kefauver to Orgill, April 25, 1957, Orgill Papers: *Memphis Press-Scimitar,* March 8, 20, April 2, 3, 26, Aug. 8, Sept. 5, 1958; Hugh Davis Graham, *Crisis In Print: Desegregation and the Press in Tennessee* (Nashville: Vanderbilt Univ. Press, 1967), 276–77; Frank E. Smith, *Congressman From Mississippi* (New York: Pantheon, 1964), 250–51.

have apportioned the funds among the various local school systems on a basis of average daily attendance. Thus Memphis with 76 percent of the pupils would receive 76 percent of the money. Instead, the county commissioners gave the city system only 50 percent and held so stubbornly to their unjust distribution that the city school system felt compelled to sue the county in the courts (The school system won). Consolidation of the two governments and the school systems would clearly have prevented the bitter and unnecessary controversy. Orgill therefore made metropolitan consolidation a main objective of his reelection campaign.[33]

The challenge to Orgill in the 1959 mayor's race came not from the old Crump crowd but from the one commissioner who also claimed to be a reformer, Henry Loeb. Open and unembarrassed in his youthful enthusiasm and backslapping exuberance, Loeb wanted to be the star of city government. Loeb had no separate municipal program of his own, he simply wanted to be mayor. He thought Edmund Orgill could be beaten because of his reputation as an integrationist, a city manager advocate, and the mayor who permitted the Ford assembly plant to move out of Memphis. He felt so confident that he even refused to accept Orgill's offer to withdraw from the campaign in return for his signed agreement to work for council-manager government and other reform goals. Loeb preferred the pleasure of beating Orgill in a spirited contest.[34]

How the election would have turned out can never be known because Orgill was forced to retire from the campaign by a blocked artery and two serious operations.[35] Memphians would probably never erect a bronze statue in his honor, but Mayor Orgill had been as exceptional as E. H. Crump. While the boss had perfected the old political arts of personal charm so well that the citizens permitted

33. *Memphis Press-Scimitar,* Jan. 1, May 20, 1959; the county commissioners were supported by one of Crump's private acts making Shelby County an exception to the general Tennessee law that school money be distributed according to average daily attendance. The state supreme court overturned this special act in 1962, ruling in favor of the Memphis Board of Education.

34. *Memphis Press-Scimitar,* June 30, 1952, Dec. 7, 1954, March 31, 1955; interview with Dr. Henry Gotten, Aug. 30, 1973; Ross Pritchard to Orgill, March 15, 1959, Burch to Loeb, March 30, 1959, Orgill Papers.

35. *Memphis Press-Scimitar,* July 4, 6, 1959.

him to take dictatorial power, Orgill was not even a politician at all in the common meaning of the word. He never bothered to charm individuals and certainly never used the mayor's office to do a favor for any of his fellow civic reformers. Lucius Burch, for example, had contributed thousands of dollars to Orgill's campaigns, but the mayor never returned the compliment, leaving Burch to say, "He has never recommended me in the course of all these years to a single person as a lawyer. I have received no public or civic recognition as his friend and supporter. . . ."[36] Personal relationships and public acclaim were simply unimportant to a man motivated by duty and purpose. He responded to municipal causes and projects rather than to individuals and public recognition. Unlike the crafty Boss Crump, Edmund Orgill backed unpopular causes—tax increases, council-manager government, consolidation—and even cautiously supported integration. Orgill compromised so little on his principles that he would never have been a professional politician with long tenure in public office, but he did give Memphis four years of energetic reform government. He looked after details such as consolidating the many city insurance policies to save the city $100,000 and, more important, restored free discussion and aggressive leadership for solving urban problems.

By beginning the expressways, the civic center, and the medical center, Edmund Orgill had promoted conspicuous urban monuments that would surely last until the end of the century. The doctrine of urban renewal, however, would lose some of its luster and be remembered as much for its failures as its successes. After the bulldozers cleared acres of blighted neighborhoods around downtown Memphis, little except weeds grew on most of the leveled sites. Federal money could bulldoze decay and slums but never stem the drift of retail business to attractive regional shopping malls. The central business district declined until it was little more than a local shopping center. The east-west expressway also remained unfinished twenty years later, stopping at the edge of Overton Park, blocked in the courts by environmentalists. If urban redevelopment failed to

36. Burch to Meeman, March 23, 1959, Meeman Papers.

deliver on all its promises, the flaw was not simply with Orgill's administration but with the renewal doctrine of urban experts.

Orgill demonstrated a new style of leadership that would be nationally applauded during the sixties, when Ivan Allen of Atlanta stepped forward as another liberal mayor in the urban South. Both mayors were establishment businessmen who stepped outside their class and emerged as local leaders seeking to help their community through the crisis of desegregation. Both were elected by a coalition of blacks and businessmen from the chamber of commerce. Each saw the wisdom of change and the necessity of avoiding race as a political issue so that community trust and reason, essential for the working of democracy, might be preserved. Orgill understood that most groups—whether blacks, labor, or business—put self-interest before the community good. By appealing to both the general public and civic-minded individuals from each interest group, he sought to lead Memphis toward a better community. He and his fellow reformers maintained interracial discussions and avoided violence during his four years in office. Because of his convictions, Orgill was never completely successful as a politician, but the civic reformers were certain that a finer statesman would never be mayor of Memphis.

6.

Restyling Local Government

Mayor Orgill's withdrawal threatened to idle the most extensive campaign machinery ever assembled by the local reformers. In the spring of 1959, Edmund Orgill had taken Ed Dalstrom, Lucius Burch, W. M. Barr, and a sack of hamburgers out for lunch at the office of a local chemical manufacturer, Dr. Stanley J. Buckman. The North Dakota-born Buckman had earned a Ph.D. at the University of Minnesota and then moved south to work in the chemical industry. He founded Buckman Laboratories in 1945 and built it into a diversified chemical corporation with foreign branches. Buckman had proven his superb administrative ability, and the Orgill group wanted him to manage the mayor's reelection campaign. The surprised Buckman had for years been one of Orgill's friends in the chamber of commerce and had a high regard for the mayor (although he did think Orgill's friend Estes Kefauver too liberal), but Buckman had avoided politics and certainly had no experience running a political campaign. After first declining, Buckman finally yielded a few days later at a Tennessee Club luncheon where Edward B. LeMaster, Edward Meeman, Albert Rickey, and Sam Hollis insisted that it was his civic duty to accept. Once committed, Buckman promptly installed a bank of telephones at his company headquarters and instructed his workers to phone everyone in the city, street by street, locating Orgill supporters and campaign volunteers. The quickly recruited volunteer army of 3,000 was the envy of all other politicians, and even if Orgill were not to run himself, it seemed a waste that the volunteers should never be used. So Edward Meeman proposed that the Orgill group be turned into a citizens association for good government.[1]

The Orgill Committee reorganized itself as the Citizens Association, which would query all municipal candidates on principles relating to good government and then endorse those who agreed to work for a new form of city government, city-county consolidation, comprehensive planning, annexation of suburban areas, reappraisals of property assessment, and a small-scale Hatch Act. To this list of good government objectives, the Citizens Association added an endorsement of segregation "by all lawful means." Most of the Orgill group were integrationists privately, but they agreed that in order to win the white vote a candidate had to affirm his support for racial separatism, especially during an election in which young blacks had deserted the Orgill coalition and were waging a strong ethnic campaign for a seat on the city commission and for an end to all racial discrimination.

Following the death of J. E. Walker in 1958, the black Democratic leadership had fallen to the younger generation, which dismissed the old coalition politics as paternalistic and wrote off Edmund Orgill as "well-meaning" but "ineffectual."[2] These were educated attorneys from the middle class, including Russell Sugarmon, Jr., the Harvard-trained son of a local realtor, A. W. Willis, Jr., the Wisconsin-educated son of a local executive of Universal life insurance, and Benjamin Hooks, the son of an old Memphis family of photographers and a graduate of De Paul University Law School. They were impatient with white civic reformers and determined to use the municipal campaign as a means of increasing black awareness, pushing racial integration, and winning political power. The

1. Interview with Stanley J. Buckman, June 25, 1973; the reformers' Good Local Government League, organized for the 1956 state elections, had collapsed after its defeat at the polls.
2. Interview with Russell Sugarmon, Jr., Sanitation Strike Archives; William E. Wright, *Memphis Politics: A Study in Bloc Voting* (New York: McGraw-Hill, 1962).

black ticket included two attorneys, Russell Sugarmon, Jr. and Benjamin Hooks, and two ministers, Reverend Roy Love and Reverend Henry Clay Bunton, men who attracted the support of the entire black leadership. Black Memphians united to raise a $20,000 campaign fund. They organized mass rallies with such speakers as Dr. Martin Luther King, Jr. and generally made unregistered blacks feel uncomfortable and out of step with their community. The black community threatened to turn out in record numbers, and they would win if the white majority scattered its vote among competing white candidates.

In a racially divided community, the reformers were afraid to endorse civil rights. Orgill's recent gubernatorial campaign failure had made them more reluctant to endorse racial justice during an election year. Their recruitment of Stanley Buckman had been an attempt to make a more conservative appeal with a campaign manager who had never been identified with liberal Democratic politics. Buckman, as leader of the new Citizens Association, recruited editor Frank Ahlgren of the segregationist *Commercial Appeal,* promising that the good government group was no longer a liberal Kefauver organization. "While there, of course, are Kefauver supporters in our association," Buckman wrote, "it is definitely not a movement to create support for Kefauver in his next campaign. The writer is not a Kefauver supporter and many other current members are of the same thought."[3]

Certainly Buckman's group never seriously considered forming a racially integrated ticket in 1959 but willingly became the "white man's" candidates. In forming their slate they even signed up two old machine politicians. Commissioners Claude Armour and John T. Dwyer were offered support from the Citizens Association if they initialed an agreement to work for the nine-point reform program. So Armour, Dwyer, Henry Loeb, and two new politicians— James W. Moore and William W. Farris—signed an agreement to work for the Orgill goals and became the candidates of the Citizens

3. Stanley Buckman to Frank Ahlgren, Aug. 3, 1959, Citizens Association Papers, Mississippi Valley Collection.

Association. As the slate with the strongest backing, including endorsements by both the *Commercial Appeal* and the *Memphis Press-Scimitar,* they won acceptance as the "white unity" ticket, the candidates who were surest to defeat the black politicians. The Citizens Association ticket won overwhelming majorities. Whites undoubtedly rallied to the strong slate more to prevent the election of black officials than to elect candidates who had endorsed good government. But the Citizens Association took credit for the victory and remained organized to see that these officeholders kept their promises.

With political success the Citizens Association became the dynamic Memphis reform group, leaving the Civic Research Committee to fade away. Research and analysis could simply no longer compete with the excitement of electing candidates who would enact the association's program.[4] The Citizens Association offered everyone a place in its permanent precinct organization, which quickly saw action again in the elections for Shelby County government and for the Tennessee state legislature. Campaigning for a winning organization offered satisfaction and respectability. The association, which endorsed former supporters of Crump such as Claude Armour and Buddy Dwyer, was less controversial than the old Civic Research Committee with its ties to Kefauver, blacks, and liberalism. Cautious men who would never have dared join CRC now affiliated with the Citizens Association; even Henry Loeb joined. Edward Meeman had finally achieved a major goal—a victorious reform organization supported by the establishment.

Few blacks ever filled out applications for the Citizens Association. The association did drop its segregation plank after the 1959 election, and a few moderate blacks joined, but the organization took no further interest in racial matters and never included the new leaders of the black community. Orgill, Meeman, and Burch had separated their concern for blacks from their politics, supporting desegregation through the Memphis Committee on Community Relations and using the Citizens Association only to support white

4. Peterson, *The Day of the Mugwump,* 322.

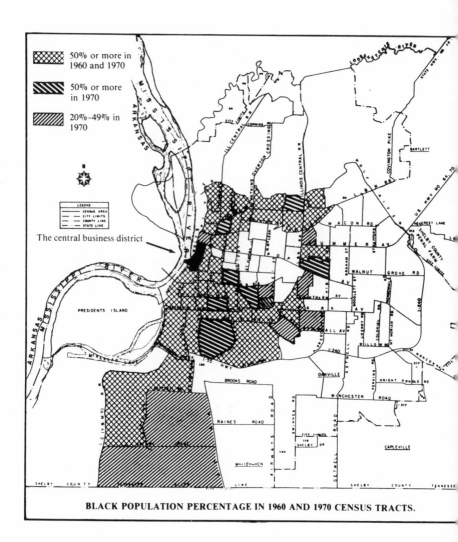

The central business district

BLACK POPULATION PERCENTAGE IN 1960 AND 1970 CENSUS TRACTS.

Legend:
- 50% or more in 1960 and 1970
- 50% or more in 1970
- 20%–49% in 1970

candidates who endorsed the goals of good government, such as city-county consolidation and reassessment of Shelby County real estate.[5]

Capricious property assessments had persisted despite three studies exposing discriminatory taxing of real estate in Shelby County. City and county tax men had appraised so erratically or maliciously that a piece of property might be listed in the tax books at any price from 20 to more than 100 percent of its market value. In 1957 the Civic Research Committee published a first tax study demonstrating the inequities and calling for tax equalization. The Tennessee Taxpayers Association confirmed the report and further demonstrated the incompetence of Shelby County tax assessment with another study published in 1959. But not until completion in 1960 of a third investigation by the Memphis Chamber of Commerce and the election of George C. LaManna as Shelby County tax assessor did equalization gain much momentum.[6]

Crump's tax assessor for the past twenty years was defeated by George LaManna and the Citizens Association in 1960. LaManna had not been a civic reformer, but neither had he been a machine politician. Born in Pennsylvania, he had come to Tennessee for a legal education and remained on to enter Memphis law practice in 1929. As an attorney employed in real estate transfers, he had seen the inequities of tax assessments. Three times LaManna had campaigned for local office unsuccessfully, but this time he rode the wave of reform, attacking inequitable tax appraisals, promising to hire professional appraisers, and supporting the consolidation of city and county assessors' offices. Backed by the chamber of commerce and the Citizens Association, LaManna made reform assessments, employing first J. Edward Rountrey, former tax assessor of Richmond, Virginia, to conduct a training program for the office staff, and then in 1963 paying a real estate consultant firm in St.

5. *Memphis Press-Scimitar,* Sept. 11, 1959; Oct. 18, 1960, Dec. 12, 1961; Minute Books, Citizens Association Papers.

6. Civic Research Committee, "Report of the Local Tax Structure Committee on Real Estate Assessments in the City of Memphis" (Memphis: CRC, 1957) (mimeographed); W. H. Brandon to Edmund Orgill, March 7, 1958, Orgill to Pete Sisson, Nov. 17, 1958, Orgill Papers; Chamber of Commerce, "A Program of Tax Equalization" (Memphis: Chamber, 1960).

Louis almost a million dollars to photograph, inspect, and appraise the value of every piece of real estate in Shelby County. By 1965 Shelby County had accurate tax appraising, and its assessor, La-Manna, had become a professional with a qualified staff.[7]

The chamber of commerce had joined the Citizens Association in an activist role, pushing not only property reassessments but also city-county consolidation. In September 1959 the chamber appointed a study group on metropolitan government, the Galbreath Committee, thereby clearly departing from traditional efforts to keep politics behind the scenes. Pressure from Edmund Orgill and his business friends, such as R. A. Trippeer and Edward LeMaster, combined with the insistence of the national Chamber of Commerce that businessmen enter politics to stop the drift towards socialism, finally pushed the local chamber into political involvement. The chamber appointed the consolidation committee and publicized the need for a twentieth century government that could eliminate overlapping city and county functions, prevent the economic strangulation of the central city, and save the taxpayer's money. For a year and a half the chamber studied and discussed consolidation, and then it appointed a new action committee of distinguished attorneys and businessmen—including Edmund Orgill (whose health and civic vigor had been restored)—to bring the issue before the voters.[8]

The Special Committee on Local Government Organization began meeting in May 1961. It quickly called for local government to establish an official charter commission to write a constitution for the consolidated metropolitan government. The two daily newspapers and the city commission supported the move toward metropolitan government. But the county commission and especially Commissioner David Harsh objected that elsewhere voters had almost uni-

7. Interview with George C. LaManna, Jan. 2, 1975; interview with Edmund Orgill, Sept. 2, 1974; *Memphis Press-Scimitar,* July 20, Aug. 1, 1960, Nov. 8, 1961; *Commercial Appeal,* April 29, 1963, June 20, 1964; George C. LaManna, "The Duties and Responsibilities of the Assessor," *Assessors Journal* 8 (Oct. 1973), 31-34.
8. Orgill to R. A. Trippeer, Jan. 4, 1957, Orgill to David N. Harsh, Aug. 7, 1957, Burch to A. I. Davies, April 6, 1959, Orgill to Members of Chamber of Commerce, June 15, 1959, Orgill Papers; A. I. Davies to Members, Dec. 7, 1959, Citizens Association Papers; *Commercial Appeal,* Sept. 20, 1959; *Memphis Press-Scimitar,* March 5, 1960, May 1, 1961; *Memphis Business,* May 1961.

versally rejected every attempt to adopt the new form and that in the few cases where it had been approved, taxes had increased. In a delaying tactic, Harsh refused even to consider appointing a charter commission until the chamber of commerce drafted a specific document describing the nature and exact organization of the government it desired.[9] The special committee responded to the Harsh opposition by printing a public relations booklet—the "Shelby Unity Plan"— describing the friction, duplication, and unrepresentative nature of the existing government. It noted, "Consolidated government would put an end to the friction, bickering, petty jealousies, and competition presently existent in our multiple governmental structure." The committee then drafted a charter for unified government, a forty-nine page document providing for a mayor-council form and election of two-thirds of the council by districts, as blacks and rural people wished, rather than at large as the chamber of commerce preferred.[10]

The special committee published its proposed metropolitan constitution on February 15, 1962, and two weeks later the city and the county separately named five individuals to an official charter commission that would draft a final constitution for the voters to accept or reject in a fall referendum. The five city appointees from the chamber's special committee were Walter Armstrong, Jr., Stanley J. Buckman, Albert C. Rickey, J. Thurston Roach, and Russel S. Wilkinson, while only one of the county choices could be considered a strong advocate of consolidation. The two attorneys on the county list—Lake Hays and David Hanover—were closely associated with the county commissioners: one had been employed by the county for twenty-five years and the other had an appointment to handle condemnation suits in the acquisition of rights-of-way for expressways through Shelby County. The black appointee, Lieutenant George W. Lee, an insurance executive and prominent Republican, was an old associate of the Crump organization but, more important, would place black demands for political power above any de-

9. Orgill, Minute Book, May 11-July 11, 1961, Orgill Papers; Albert C. Rickey, "City County Consolidation: The Inside Story," *The Egyptians* (1972), 1-15.

10. Manuscript Charter, Orgill Papers; *Commercial Appeal,* Feb. 16, 1962; *Memphis Business,* March 1962.

sire for a consolidated government. Mrs. Ellen Davis Rodgers, a Jeffersonian Democrat who lived on a 2,000-acre plantation in the county, opposed consolidation. Only Kemmons Wilson, chairman of the board of Holiday Inns of America, enthusiastically supported consolidation and would cast his decisive vote with the five city appointees.[11]

The new committee began work in March amid hostile county criticism of metropolitan government. County Court Squire Paul W. Barret mailed out 8,000 copies of a rightwing attack on the unity plan. He labeled it "a socialist scheme to destroy local government." The rural politicians and the small-town newspapers such as the *Millington Star* expressed fear that their people's independence and freedom would be crushed by a big Shelby County government so remote that the voice of a citizen could not be heard.[12]

The most divisive issue within the charter commission meetings was the chamber of commerce drive to elect all twelve metropolitan councilmen without single-member districts, thus rejecting the earlier compromise of the special committee on district representation. The chamber representatives insisted that four councilmen be elected at large from the central city, four at large from the area outside Memphis, and four by county-wide vote. Rural and small-town people feared that they would be unable to elect a single representative because suburban Whitehaven could dominate the elections outside the central city, while Memphis voters would easily claim the other eight seats. The black minority understood this selection process as anti-Negro. Actually, the decision represented the chamber's abstract political theory, shared by reformers such as Lucius Burch, that at-large elections would avoid corrupt ward politics and insure the election of men who would never put the needs of their own district above the welfare of the entire community. To be sure, at-large campaigns were expensive and more likely to elect financially able candidates from the chamber of commerce, but not all chamber representatives sought to exclude blacks from office. Dr.

11. *Commercial Appeal,* March 2, 3, 1962; *Memphis Press-Scimitar,* March 2, 1962.
12. *Millington Star,* Feb. 22, 1962; *Commercial Appeal,* March 6, 1962; Sheriff M. A. Hinds, scrapbooks, Mississippi Valley Collection.

Stanley Buckman, for example, wanted blacks on the metropolitan council. He worked unsuccessfully to have the commission name the entire first council and include two blacks who would establish a tradition of black representation. But even Buckman could never understand the political necessity of compromise and single-member districts to secure the victory of metropolitan government.[13]

The black leadership in Memphis believed that any gains in efficiency from metropolitan government were insufficient to recommend a system which seemed designed to continue black exclusion from local office. "My constituents feel that their only hope for survival is a council based on districts," said Lieutenant George W. Lee, the only black member of the commission. "I can't get away from that and keep faith with my constituents." NAACP President Jesse Turner said, "Since everybody is running at large, the Negro doesn't have much of a chance unless he's one that the whites will accept." The NAACP voted unanimously to oppose the metropolitan charter and argued in its propaganda that consolidation would move government farther from black people and promote dictatorship.[14]

The chamber of commerce stressed the notion that elimination of governmental friction by the metropolitan plan would result in reduced government expense, permitting taxes to be lowered and thereby luring enough industry to Shelby County to provide jobs and prosperity for all. The president of the chamber of commerce, Edward LeMaster, assured Memphians that industry would be attracted if the city adopted the new charter and created the image of a progressive metropolitan area. Stanley J. Buckman revealed that new industry currently preferred other Southern cities because of governmental instability in Memphis. "We cannot get decisions from your multiple-headed governmental structure," industrialists had complained to Buckman. "Everyone passes the buck. . . . There is too much bickering between the County Commission, County Court and City Commission. In the face of all this, how can we tell what will happen in the future?" Palmer Brown III, president of a

13. Stanley J. Buckman to Meeman, June 5, 1962; Burch to Alexander Gladney, June 20, 1962, Meeman Papers; *Commercial Appeal,* May 19, 1962; *Collierville Herald,* July 19, Aug. 30, 1962.
14. *Memphis Press-Scimitar,* May 30, Sept. 6, 1962.

cotton bale bagging company, added: "I am a businessman—not a politician. It distresses me to see politics injected into the consolidation charter referendum. This is a business matter and should be decided on business principles."[15]

The business community, working through the Citizens Association, organized to defeat those old county politicians who opposed consolidation. The Citizens Association with its 700 members, its precinct organization, and its large advertising budget, publicized the negativism of Crump's former officials and Commissioner David Harsh in particular. The reformers were prepared to endorse Commissioner Rudolph Jones if he agreed to abandon his old alliance with Harsh and join the "metro" forces, but he refused and so both Crump men on the three-member Shelby County commission were targeted for defeat. The reformers drafted a Front Street cotton man, Jack W. Ramsay, to head their county commission ticket. The cotton men were clannish, and Ramsay was one of the few to participate in civic reform. He had never joined the Civic Research Committee, to be sure, but he had supported Edmund Orgill's election in 1955 and served as president of the Citizens Association. He was a modest, reluctant candidate who entered politics only because his fellow reformers drafted him and waged the campaign for him against David Harsh. The metro ticket headed by Ramsay won the August elections, easily defeating the old organization and giving the reformers control of county government.[16]

The defeat of David Harsh and Rudolph Jones greatly encouraged hopes of victory for a consolidation referendum in the fall election. But Shelby County voters were fickle, easier to arouse against Crump's officials than to persuade that they ought to support metropolitan reform. When the voters returned to the polls in November, Jack Ramsay and his metropolitan forces could not even win a majority for metro in the central city; outside the city, metro was voted down three to one. Memphis voters, like those of Nashville, Knoxville, Louisville, Cleveland, St. Louis, and Seattle, had rejected consolidation.

15. *Commercial Appeal,* Nov. 5, 1962; *Millington Star,* Aug. 16, 1962.
16. Interview with Jack Ramsay, Sept. 9, 1974; *Memphis Press-Scimitar,* Oct. 18, 1960, Aug. 3, Nov. 7, 1962.

The defeated advocates of metropolitan government intended to try again four years later, but with the political defeat of county politician David Harsh, city-county friction became less annoying than internal city commission strife. Mayor Henry Loeb (1960–1963) presided over a fractious administration. He proclaimed his segregationist views loudly enough to alienate the entire black community, and he turned furiously on those who dared to criticize him. He played the demagogue against taxes, opposing construction of the new stadium, the civic center, the fine arts center, and hastening of the expressway construction.[17] When Loeb decided not to run for reelection in 1963, the race narrowed to a contest between Commissioner William Farris, the Citizens Association candidate, and the city judge, William B. Ingram, Jr., who had no prominent support. Ingram had risen to fame by a personal feud with the police department, insisting that officers prove their charges and dismissing 46.7 percent of the traffic cases because police testimony seemed unsatisfactory. He explained his purpose as the preservation of individual freedom from arbitrary and illegal police power. But when he ordered his own court clerk and his court officer arrested for contempt, the establishment diagnosed Ingram as troubled by his own personality disorder rather than by violations of principle.[18]

Judge Ingram campaigned for mayor in 1963 without billboards, paid workers, or an advertising budget. He took his little portable loudspeaker to the shopping centers, spoke in all the small black churches and all the white working-class organizations, appearing to be a segregationist to whites and an integrationist to blacks, but always identifying with the little man against the establishment—the press, the police department, and the chamber of commerce. With the votes of blacks, workers, and some middle-class conservatives who feared that the Citizens Association candidate might raise taxes, he won election as mayor in 1963. Ingram represented a revolution in Memphis politics, a unique mayor elected without establishment support. Both Crumpites and reformers had come from

17. *Memphis Press-Scimitar,* Oct. 9, 1962; *Commercial Appeal,* Feb. 17, 20, April 3, 1963.
18. *Memphis Press-Scimitar,* May 28, June 18, 1959, Jan. 10, Oct. 26, 1961, Nov. 8, 1963; *Commercial Appeal,* Oct. 22, 1963.

the same country club society. But Ingram and his appointees were socially unknown to the local upper classes, who viewed the new mayor with alarm. Ingram intended to dominate the city commission but was quickly frustrated by the four other commissioners. He fought on, keeping city government in constant controversy and continuing to lash out at the establishment. Ingram even called the chamber of commerce a "morgue."[19]

Little more than a month after Ingram took office, Lucius Burch wrote Frank Ahlgren that the city hall troubles provided an opportunity for changing the form of municipal government:

> The situation existing in the City Commission is going to result in four years of anarchy unless Ingram is able to obtain control of the Commissioners. Either will be bad. I have known Ingram for many years. He is psychologically incapable of taking part in any relationship wherein his own views and feelings must be compromised. He is intelligent and has an intuitive awareness of what pleases the masses. But, what I am concerned with is not Judge Ingram and I mention this only to justify the prophesy of parlous times ahead.
>
> What is now highlighted are the inherent weaknesses and insufficiencies of our form of municipal government. Some good can be made to come out of the chaos if the example spurs the electorate to reform the city charter, which is now easily possible under the home rule amendment to the Constitution.
>
> What I am proposing for your consideration and support is the formation of a truly representative body of citizens to undertake a serious study of our charter and the various forms of city government with the purpose of finally arriving at a consensus as to the best form of government for this city and then supplying the political leadership and effort to institute the form of government agreed upon as desirable.
>
> To accomplish such a program a number of things are necessary. First, both newspapers would have to be active participants rather than reporters in the study, decision, and action. There are certain areas of community life in which I believe both papers must be cooperative as movers and doers. The good that comes from this in the proper areas is best demonstrated by the Memphis Committee on Community Relations. What has been done here to establish the best record of any city in the country in handling racial matters would have been absolutely impossible without you and Ed Meeman. . . .

19. *Commercial Appeal,* Jan. 17, 23, March 20, 1964; interview with Frances Coe, Mississippi Valley Collection.

112

Second, those participating as members of the study committee would have to be truly representative of the power structure of the city. This would insure that all partisan viewpoints were accommodated in the study and there would then be a sufficiently broad base for political activity to accomplish the desired result. To select the right membership of the committee is not as simple as it sounds because events of the recent past have shown that what we generally believe to be the power structure of the city is not now in many cases politically effective. The results of the election respecting consolidation and Ingram's election are examples that come to mind.[20]

Frank Ahlgren did detest Mayor Ingram, but the editor thought Burch's timing a bit premature. He said that complacent Memphians would require a bit more of Ingram's administration before they could be startled into serious reconsideration of the form of government. So Ahlgren sought to arouse Memphians by taking every opportunity to tell his readers that Ingram had put local government in "shameful disarray," had "wrecked the good image of Memphis," and had "undermined confidence in the city government." But for more than a year Ahlgren hesitated to call for a change in government.[21]

In the fall of 1965 Ahlgren finally instructed his brightest city hall reporter, Jack H. Morris, who had studied local government in graduate school at the University of Wisconsin, to write a series of ten articles on urban troubles, the existing forms of city government, and the need to replace the antique commission form in Memphis.[22] After the impressive series appeared in the *Commercial Appeal*, Lucius Burch stepped forward to invite eight Memphis leaders, including black and labor representatives, to meet with Jack Morris and himself at the Wolf River Society to plan a campaign for changing the form of government. The group followed the plan Burch had earlier recommended to editor Frank Ahlgren, drafting a list of 277 prominent local leaders from labor, business, education, religion, ethnic, and civic groups, to whom special invitations were sent, inviting them to attend public meetings at which

20. Burch to Frank Ahlgren, Feb. 19, 1964, Orgill Papers.
21. Ahlgren to Burch, Feb. 20, 1964, Orgill Papers; *Commercial Appeal,* March 22, April 2, June 28, 1964.
22. *Ibid.,* Oct. 17–26, 1965.

twenty-five citizens would be elected to serve on a Program of Progress committee to draft a new charter for Memphis. To insure some control over these elections in the December meeting, the Burch group organized two tickets of candidates balanced by representatives from the major opinion groups. Only Ingram supporters and those who had enthusiastically supported Crump were excluded.[23] The resulting twenty-five winners included many distinguished individuals representing a cross-section of Memphis but no leaders from the old Civic Research Committee. The voluntary absence of the old reformers from the Program of Progress (POP) committee reflected their political demise at the very time their ideas about good government were winning.

The old reformers had hitched their hopes for ending the commission form of government to a committee composed largely of blacks, Republicans, and businessmen.[24] The six black politicians and NAACP leaders—Russell Sugarmon, Jr., A. W. Willis, Jr., Jesse H. Turner, Dr. Vasco Smith, H. T. Lockard, and Reverend Alexander Gladney —were hostile to the old commission form, which excluded minorities from city government by requiring at-large elections for the five commission seats. Blacks could be counted on to support a new council with district seats. Just as blacks could be assured control of seats in their own neighborhoods, so could Republicans dominate districts in the wealthier east Memphis suburbs. In the past, Republicans had elected no spokesman to the commission, but local politics was changing rapidly as the establishment shifted towards the Republican party. While no prominent white establishment Democrat had been elected to the Program of Progress committee, five Republican party leaders—Gwen Awsumb, Lewis Donelson III, Alex W. Dann, Dan Kuykendall, and Keith Spurrier—were selected to reflect new Republican influence. As members of the reform Citi-

23. Jonathan I. Wax, "Program of Progress, A Step Into the Present," (senior thesis, Princeton Univ., 1968), 37; Jack H. Morris, "Chronology of a Charter," manuscript in POP Papers, Mississippi Valley Collection.

24. Not included in the three big categories were three establishment clergymen (Reverend Dix Archer, Dr. Paul Tudor Jones, and Rabbi James A. Wax), three Democrats associated with labor (Tommy Powell, Anthony Sabella, and Cliff Tuck), and a political science professor, E. C. Buell.

zens Association, these Republicans could be counted on to support a council reform, and as minority party members they could support black demands for district seats. Chamber of commerce leaders C. Whitney Brown, Sam Cooper, Robert Galloway, Downing Pryor, Robert G. Snowden, Wallace Witmer, and Walter Armstrong, who wanted to preserve the reformer belief in at-large elections nevertheless forced a compromise—a thirteen-seat council divided into seven districts and six at-large seats.

After thirty-five meetings during the next six months, the POP committee completed a mayor-council charter for Memphis. The reformers' old hope for a city manager never even had a serious discussion. Over the years a local consensus developed for a strong mayor. The *Commercial Appeal* had advocated a mayor rather than a manager, the metropolitan consolidation charter had called for a mayor, and when the Program for Progress began its meetings, blacks, Republicans, and labor representatives considered only a mayor for city executive.[25]

The final draft of the charter was approved by the POP committee on June 2, 1966, and the Chamber of Commerce and the NAACP then endorsed the plan. Mayor Ingram, who regarded the charter as an establishment plot against him, reluctantly agreed to a referendum that he hoped to turn against his enemies. But in November the establishment, with the support of blacks and labor, outvoted Ingram and the opponents of change. On election day 60 percent of the voters approved the new style of city government.[26]

The city commission had finally been defeated, twenty years after Edward Meeman, Edmund Orgill, and Lucius Burch began organizing for charter reform. The old reformers were disappointed in their failure to obtain a city-manager executive, but they took satisfaction in having finally divided legislative and executive functions and in having secured a part-time council that could intelligently represent the major interests of Memphis. The reformers were generally pleased by the voters' selections for the first council. Three

25. Jonathan Wax, "Program of Progress," 104.
26. Jack H. Morris, "Chronology of a Charter," 16; Erwin C. Buell, "How the Commission Form Lost," *American City* 83 (July 1968), 118.

blacks were elected along with establishment whites selected by the business community and the Citizens Association, which the old reformers no longer controlled.[27] Orgill, Meeman, and Burch could congratulate itself on having secured the cooperation of blacks and whites in modernizing local government and electing a promising council, but it lamented the growing polarization of the races and the failure of Memphians to unite behind a reasonable choice for mayor.

The Memphis establishment stood united in the goal of blocking Mayor Ingram's reelection but split four ways in choosing a candidate to oppose him. The black establishment endorsed the Negro attorney A. W. Willis, Jr. The Orgill-Burch group backed a young civic reformer, Hunter Lane, Jr., whose father had been one of the original directors of the Civic Research Committee and who himself had been the one city commissioner who campaigned actively for the POP charter. The cautious *Commercial Appeal* and much of the Citizens Association had endorsed the personable Sheriff William Morris. The establishment conservatives backed former mayor Henry Loeb, who had preserved his image as a segregationist and could win no black votes. Loeb easily beat these three rivals and then won in the resulting runoff election against Mayor Ingram.[28]

The victory of Henry Loeb, the most conservative mayoral candidate, reflected a shift of white Memphians during the early sixties. Memphians were voting for the reform proposed by Burch, Orgill, and Meeman but not for their moderate politics. Moderation had been rejected by the white community and also by the black. Together, black and white voters gave Hunter Lane, the moderate candidate of Burch, Orgill, and Meeman, less than 7 percent of the vote. White Memphians apparently wanted to abandon both the old commission form of government and Orgill's moderate style of politics. Black leaders were equally intent on abandoning the commission form and the white liberal politicians. They advanced black candidates and refused to support a white liberal in the initial mayor's race. After the defeat of A. W. Willis, all blacks shifted their

27. *Memphis Press-Scimitar,* Nov. 3, 1967.
28. Loeb led in the primary with 47,000 votes, followed by Ingram with 36,000, Morris with 30,000, Willis 18,000, and Lane 8,000 (*Commercial Appeal,* Oct. 6, 1967).

support to Mayor Ingram in the runoff. Almost 90 percent of whites backed Henry Loeb, electing him the mayor of Memphis. Race relations under the new government proved to be social dynamite, precisely what the reformers had always hoped to avoid.

7.

Black Leadership and Desegregation

While the Citizens Association concentrated on reorganizing local government, black civil rights leaders were becoming frustrated and impatient. All the easy battles against glaring examples of racial discrimination—involving buses, libraries, lunch counters, white public schools—were won, but still poverty and prejudice persisted. Civic reformers who had helped in past struggles for desegregation seemed less willing to continue in the war against black poverty and discrimination. Black leadership now felt a loss of civil rights momentum, a rising anger at the more subtle forms of discrimination and a loss of faith in the moderate tactics that had worked in the past.

The new militancy marked a break from the moderate black leadership of the past. The Memphis NAACP had been especially restrained in pushing change. Led by prudent realists, it had been keenly aware of the prejudice of white Mississippians who had carried their racism with them when they moved north to Memphis. When the Supreme Court ruled school segregation unconstitutional in 1954, the local NAACP applied no pressure to the public schools but instead went to Memphis State College and asked for the admission of black students. When Memphis State refused to desegregate, the NAACP filed its first civil rights suit in 1955 and pursued the evasive college administrators, who delayed with court maneuvers. The college admitted no black students for four more years.[1]

The Memphis NAACP moved very slowly in bringing court action against other public institutions. When federal district judges ruled segregation on Montgomery buses unconstitutional in 1956, a controversial employee of the Memphis post office, O. Z. Evers, who was not identified with the NAACP, filed a desegregation suit against the Memphis bus company. A black banker and NAACP board member, Jesse Turner, began a desegregation suit against the public libraries in 1958. The NAACP filed a suit regarding use of the zoo and park in 1959, but not until the student sit-ins of 1960 did the organization begin a suit against the Memphis Board of Education.[2]

The NAACP had won only the case involving integration at Memphis State when the southern sit-in movement spread to the city and brought rapid desegregation in 1960. Forty-one students at Le-Moyne and Owen colleges were arrested on the afternoon of Saturday, March 19, for entering two public libraries. A wave of sit-ins and arrests continued as students also entered the Pink Palace Museum, Brooks Memorial Art Gallery, and Overton Park. Some sat at downtown lunch counters and took front seats on Memphis Transit buses. The NAACP and the local black ministers united behind the demonstrators. They collected "freedom donations" during church services to pay the fines of nonviolent students who faced charges of disorderly conduct, loitering, and threatening to disturb the peace, all because they had dared to seek racial equality by using the public facilities. Black adults supported the students financially and joined in the protest by boycotting the downtown merchants in a campaign which continued sporadically for a year and a half.[3]

The sit-in movement brought renewed vigor to the local Committee on Community Relations, which had been organized to avert racial trouble. Amid news of black demonstrations and white violence

1. *Memphis World,* June 4, 1954, July 19, 1958; *Tri-State Defender,* June 4, 11, 1955; *Memphis Press-Scimitar,* Sept. 15, 1958, March 31, April 3, 1960.

2. *Memphis Press-Scimitar,* June 5, 1956, Aug. 15, 1958, Jan. 5, 1959.

3. U.S. Commission on Civil Rights, *Hearings Before the U.S. Commission on Civil Rights, Memphis, June, 1962* (Washington: GPO, 1963), 111-2; *Commercial Appeal,* March 19, 20, 22, 1960; Tucker, *Black Pastors and Leaders,* 113-18.

in other Southern cities during the fall of 1958, Lucius Burch had sent out a call to individual members of the black and white power elite asking for a new bi-racial committee to provide reliable communication between the races and to provide moderate leadership for preserving law and order during the desegregation crisis. Burch's call attracted more than fifty, including both newspaper editors, the chamber of commerce leadership, Mayor Edmund Orgill's friends, and the black establishment. In sending out white invitations, Burch had largely shunned preachers and professors in favor of men of economic weight who could exert influence in shaping community decisions. The Memphis Committee on Community Relations (MCCR) had been designed to be less a debating society than a problem-solving group that would focus on specific immediate troubles and negotiate effective remedies.[4]

The MCCR began cautiously. It divided itself into five smaller committees to study the trouble spots of public transportation, libraries, schools, recreation, and housing. Only the library committee recommended immediate desegregation in 1959. But the Memphis Public Library Board, composed entirely of men beyond seventy years of age, rejected integration, and so the MCCR actually brought no changes until the sit-in movement came to Memphis in 1960. The MCCR spokesmen then returned to the library board as well as the Memphis Transit Company and the city commission, urging that voluntary desegregation was a surer way to preserve racial good will than waiting for a desegregation order from the Supreme Court. Delay and court battles, the white committee members stressed, would only strengthen the NAACP, which led the demonstrations. So the city commission reluctantly gave in by the fall of 1960 and took steps against segregation. Buses were desegregated in September, libraries in October, and Overton Park Zoo in December.[5]

Outspoken NAACP officials who were also members of the

4. The earlier interracial committee, organized after the golf course controversy in early 1956, failed largely because conservative white members refused to attend integrated meetings with black committee members; *Commercial Appeal,* Feb. 23, March 2, 1956; *Tri-State Defender,* March 31, 1956; Lucius E. Burch, Jr. to Friend, Oct. 30, Nov. 25, 1958, Orgill Papers.

5. Burch, "Report on the Memphis Committee on Community Relations," (1959), Meeman Papers; Arthur W. McCain notes on library meeting, Arthur W.

MCCR—Russell Sugarmon, Jr., Jesse H. Turner, Dr. Vasco Smith, and A.W. Willis, Jr.—insisted that the committee must move on to assist the NAACP in desegregating the lunch counters, restaurants, and restrooms in downtown department stores. The federal courts had not yet established the right of nondiscrimination in privately owned stores, but by the summer of 1961 white members agreed to appoint a special committee and persuade the merchants to desegregate voluntarily. Attorney Lewis R. Donelson III and his committee negotiated a plan in which the merchants agreed that if the NAACP would call off its picketing and economic boycott, the stores would desegregate within sixty days after Christmas. Black leaders, and especially Jesse Turner, the new president of NAACP, thought the merchant's plan was a trick and a lie. But the merchants maintained that holiday crowds and the temporary clerks employed at Christmas could make integration much more hazardous than it would be during the slow business weeks in January and February. After much argument, moderate black ministers on the committee supported the plan and, with Jesse Turner abstaining, secured its approval by the MCCR. Turner then persuaded the NAACP to call off the boycott, and after Christmas the downtown merchants desegregated as they had promised.[6]

Public school desegregation had begun in Memphis during the same school year. The Memphis School Board had refused the MCCR's offer of assistance in working out plans. Mrs. Frances Coe, civic reformer and member of the MCCR, was the single integrationist on the school board. Mrs. Coe had won election to the board in 1955 and immediately advocated integration, but the other board members insisted that Memphis could not possibly integrate voluntarily. After the NAACP began a lawsuit, the school board planned with the NAACP a surprise school integration in the fall of 1961. Even the teachers were not informed until the night before, when

---

McCain Papers, Mississippi Valley Collection; *Tri-State Defender,* Oct. 15, 1960; *Memphis Press-Scimitar,* Oct. 14, Dec. 2, 1960.

6. Interview with Arthur W. McCain, Nov. 6, 1973; Minutes of MCCR Executive Committee, Rabbi James A. Wax Papers, personal files in Baron Hirsch Synagogue; *New York Times,* Feb. 16, 1962; the ministers who moved acceptance of the compromise were Reverend S. A. Owen and Reverend David Cunningham.

Superintendent E.C. Stimbert told his faculty, "Now tomorrow morning you are going to have some new pupils and there is nothing different about them from all the pupils you have already had. You are professional people; they are going to be your children and their parents are going to be your parents, and I know that you are going to do the good job with them that you have done with your other pupils all over the years."[7] When the thirteen black students appeared, police formed a solid blue line around the four integrated schools and prepared for white resistance that never developed. The desire of Memphis leadership to prevent disruption like that at Little Rock brought token school integration without incident and without violence.

Success in desegregating schools and department stores persuaded most white MCCR members that Memphis had made rapid progress. But the black leaders—Vasco Smith and Jesse Turner—insisted that the committee had been moving too slowly and had neglected to do anything about black employment. So an employment committee under Carl Carson and Edmund Orgill began work in 1962 to persuade local firms to hire blacks in white-collar positions. The employment committee also asked Senator Estes Kefauver to apply pressure on the Kennedy administration to insist that the federal government enforce its rule requiring nondiscrimination by Memphis companies that held government contracts. Senator Kefauver was also instructed to encourage the Civil Service Department to inform local black high schools and colleges of all civil service examinations and all federal job opportunities.[8]

Movie theaters still remained segregated in Memphis, and the NAACP leadership demanded action in 1962. A special committee headed by Lucius Burch and Dr. Vasco Smith met with the local theater managers that fall and worked out a plan to desegregate the local movies secretly. Smith selected a single black couple to attend the Malco Theatre. Nothing happened to the couple. The following week two black couples were sent. Then other theaters were integrated without any newspaper publicity. By April, 1963, Smith re-

7. Frances Coe interview, Mississippi Valley Collection.
8. Edmund Orgill and Carl Carson to Estes Kefauver, Sept. 7, 1962, Orgill Papers.

Crump's biographer, William D. Miller, looking at the Boss's statue in Overton Park (credit: *The Commercial Appeal* and The Mississippi Valley Collection).

Mister E. H. Crump followed by Mayor Watkins Overton (credit: *The Commercial Appeal* and The Mississippi Valley Collection).

Downtown traffic in November 1954 (credit: *The Commercial Appeal* and The Mississippi Valley Collection).

The Memphis skyline viewed from Riverside Drive during the flood of May 1973 (credit: *The Commercial Appeal* and The Mississippi Valley Collection).

Edward J. Meeman, editor of the *Memphis Press-Scimitar* (credit: *The Commercial Appeal* and The Mississippi Valley Collection).

The Orgill Campaign Committee of September 1955; 1) Mrs. Wells Aw-sumb, 2) Dr. Henry Gotten, 3) R.A. Trippeer, 4) Edmund Orgill, 5) William Barr, 6) George Grider, 7) Walker Wellford (credit: *The Commercial Appeal* and The Mississippi Valley Collection).

The new city commissioners in January 1956; left to right, Henry Loeb, Claude A. Armour, Mayor Edmund Orgill, John T. Dwyer, Stanley Dillard (credit: *The Commercial Appeal* and The Mississippi Valley Collection).

The Shelby County Commissioners in May 1958; left to right, Rudolph Jones, Dan Mitchell, David Harsh (credit: *The Commercial Appeal* and The Mississippi Valley Collection).

Civic reformers Lucius Burch, Jr., Ed Dalstrom, William Barr', Dr. Henry Gotten, and Edmund Orgill (credit: *The Commercial Appeal* and The Mississippi Valley Collection).

New directors of the Citizens Association in December 1961: front, from the left, Dr. Stanley J. Buckman, Mrs. Wells Awsumb, Morris Austin, Jack W. Ramsay; rear, from the left, J. Thurston Roach, Edmund Orgill, J.A. Beauchamp, Samuel B. Hollis (credit: *The Commercial Appeal* and The Mississippi Valley Collection).

Striking garbage workers on February 14, 1968 (credit: *The Commercial Appeal* and The Mississippi Valley Collection).

ported that fourteen theaters had been desegregated. But Smith took no joy in his work, telling the MCCR that it should all have been done a hundred years before.[9]

Perhaps Arthur W. McCain most fully reflected the common white assumption that desegregation had moved as rapidly as the white public would tolerate. McCain, an Arkansan, had been vice-president of Chase National Bank in New York City and then presided over the local Union Planters National Bank before retiring to full-time civic reform work. He had diligently worked with the employment committee to place blacks in a hundred firms. When a rare newspaper article explained the MCCR work and reproduced a photograph of McCain with Jesse Turner, the retired banker heard himself referred to as a "nigger lover" at his country club. He received anonymous mail, with one card declaring "Race-Mixing is Communism" and another saying: "Arthur, that was a good picture of Jesse Turner, not so good of you. Few white people like what you are doing. After all you aren't a true Southerner but if trouble comes the Negro won't spare your life any quicker than mine. The Negro is a fearful growing race once removed from the jungles. My yardman went to his mother's funeral in Mississippi. She had 104 grandchildren. How many have you?"[10] The hatred apparent in such mail seemed evidence to McCain that the MCCR had pushed toward rapid desegregation. When blacks complained that too little progress was being made, he and most other white leaders were puzzled.

Lucius Burch emerged as the one white who agreed with black MCCR members in the summer of 1963 that the time had come to accelerate the desegregation of Memphis. After Martin Luther King, Jr.'s successful crusade in Birmingham and the failure of MCCR's restaurant committee to persuade local owners to desegregate, Burch called upon his fellow members to abandon all delay and persuade the local white community to accept the inevitability of total

9. Burch to Vasco Smith, Oct. 16, 1962; Minutes of MCCR Membership Meeting, April 14, 1963, Wax Papers; interview with Arthur W. McCain, Nov. 6, 1973.

10. Anonymous to Arthur W. McCain, May 20, 1963, McCain Papers; interview with McCain, Nov. 6, 1973.

desegregation. In an eloquent essay letter to the executive committee, Burch said:

> It is now clear beyond argument that no public institution has the right to deny equal facility of use to any citizen because of color. The Negro citizens are naturally restive at being thwarted and delayed in the exercise of this clearly declared right. Having been successful in establishing their rights through litigation, they now seek to obtain them by "demonstrations." These so-called "demonstrations" are ancient and constitutionally authorized remedies in that all citizens have the right to assemble peaceably, to petition for the redress of their grievances, and to publicize by picketing and other legal means their contentions. There is no legal, moral, or historical basis for condemning the assertion of rights by these methods. Indeed a nation looking with pride at such vigorous precedents as Runnymede, the Boston Tea Party, and Concord Bridge must praise rather than condemn any citizen or group of citizens vigilant and active in the establishment and protection of their liberties. This is straight talk and not calculated to please or flatter or to do other than speak the truth to tough-minded men and women sufficiently concerned to band together to achieve a solution. The truth is that if the white leadership of this community does not actively concern itself with the obtaining of legally declared rights and by its prestige and influence further rather than restrain the exercise of these rights, we must expect the Negroes to exert themselves vigorously to gain those ends which have been judicially declared to be their legitimate due.
>
> The Negro leadership in this community at this time is effective and responsible. It is composed of men who have a personal stake in the continued tranquillity and future growth of the community. The Negro leaders are ministers, merchants, teachers, bankers, lawyers, etc. and they will suffer even more than their white counterparts from disorder and they have done a magnificent job in preaching responsibility and restraint to those who look to them for leadership. But they first and foremost are members of their race and have a keen sense of injustice. Moreover, they will not remain as leaders of their people without tangible exertion and perceptible progress towards the attainment of their rights. If there is a failure of their leadership, it will be replaced by more radical groups not concerned with long term and overall community consequences. . . .
>
> In the lives of most of us there are not many opportunities to play a perceptible part in the greatest of human roles—the peaceable extension of human liberty and the creation of a climate having a greater reverence for human dignity. What is done in Little Rock, Oxford, and Birmingham is a blot upon us all, but what we do here can stand as a

beacon throughout the South and indeed the world as an example of how these problems may be solved by men with courage to take a stand upon the ground as they find it and determined to do the very best they can under the circumstances that they cannot change.[11]

Burch's letter was followed by the most divisive annual membership meeting ever held by the MCCR. The black members brought in Reverend James M. Lawson, Jr. to speak for the local NAACP. The young United Methodist minister actually represented the militant wing of the organization. He had frequently denounced the national office for its caution and reluctance to endorse nonviolent direct action. The Ohio-born Lawson came to the civil rights movement through the Fellowship of Reconciliation, America's oldest pacifist organization, which taught aggressive nonviolent action against war and injustice. The fellowship had sent him south in 1958 as an organizer of nonviolent resistance to segregation. His leadership in the Nashville sit-ins in 1960 had resulted in his expulsion from the Vanderbilt Divinity School and much national publicity. Before coming to Memphis in 1962, Lawson had led in the organization of the activist Student Non-Violent Coordinating Committee, pastored a congregation in Shelbyville, Tennessee, and served on the staff of Martin Luther King's Southern Christian Leadership Conference. After coming to Memphis, he continued his work for SCLC and joined King for the 1963 campaign in Birmingham. He returned to Memphis impatient to implement direct action tactics in the Bluff City.[12]

Reverend Lawson delivered a denunciation of the white power structure and a call for repentance. "Even a blind man can see that in Memphis our vaunted progress is but the token concession designed to maintain segregation," Lawson said. "We pride ourselves on being a city of churches, but the God of the Bible does not influence either the church or the marketplace. Baal in the form of segregation is yet our God." Blacks were no longer going to accept tokenism or delaying tactics, Lawson informed the group; blacks were turning to nonviolent direct action to help themselves and also to shock the conscience of the nation and thus save the soul of Amer-

11. Burch to Members of Executive Committee, June 5, 1963, Meeman Papers.
12. Tucker, *Black Pastors and Leaders,* 119–28.

ica from the sin of segregation. "We call upon all persons of good will," Reverend Lawson declaimed, "to commit themselves now to that repentant action which can once and for all time remove the scourge of racial evil from the land."[13]

The message fell on the ears of white committee members like an insult. They understood Lawson to be saying, "you are guilty of sin. You have got to change your morals . . . or dammit, I'll make you."[14] They could see no reason to change their tactics, which had worked in the past. Certainly his urgent call for the committee to abandon its policy of quiet negotiation and publicly to support passage of President Kennedy's civil rights legislation sounded like a folly which could only undermine the influence of the MCCR. Except for Lucius Burch, no white sensed an emergency; Burch alone agreed with Lawson that the MCCR had ignored the moral aspects of segregation and should now push desegregation with a new evangelical spirit. Burch understood the black leadership's sense of urgency and realized that past failure to hold black confidence and support had contributed to the defeat of metropolitan government for Shelby County. If black cooperation were to be secured in the coming city election, then the white elite must move faster towards total desegregation. But none of the other whites agreed with Burch's analysis of the merits of supporting the Lawson proposal. None of the other whites were ready to endorse Lawson's "Freedom Manifesto." They agreed to study the document, but there was no evidence in the following weeks that the sermon produced any repentance or change of heart.

For months after the Lawson sermon, restaurant negotiations remained at an impasse. Black leaders lost faith in negotiations and prepared to picket in December 1963. A last effort began. The MCCR committee met with twenty leading restaurant men, chamber of commerce leaders, and Police Commissioner Claude Armour. The police commissioner had a reputation as a "tough guy," a career policeman, and a segregationist, but he was committed to both enforcing the law and keeping the peace. Commissioner Armour told the restaurant managers that blacks had a right to picket and

13. James M. Lawson, Jr., "A Freedom Manifesto," McCain Papers; Minutes of Membership Meeting, July 16, 1963, Wax Papers.
14. Interview with McCain, Nov. 6, 1973.

that in other cities such as Atlanta restaurants had eventually capitulated to NAACP picketing. Restaurant owners in Memphis could save thousands of dollars by voluntary and immediate desegregation. After Armour and the chamber of commerce urged desegregation and the newspaper editors guaranteed that integration would receive no newspaper publicity, the twenty largest restaurants agreed to abandon their racial policy.[15]

MCCR members congratulated themselves in 1964 on having achieved voluntary desegregation of public accommodations in Memphis before the Civil Rights Bill was approved by Congress. Desegregation, to be sure, was only nominal. Only the better restaurants cooperated, while hundreds of smaller places continued to discriminate. But a special report from the liberal Southern Regional Council described the city as "a beacon of reason and decency for the Deep South." The "striking" and "unbelievable" change resulted, the report said, from the quiet bi-racial cooperation of the black and white elite. The leaders on each side had been able to control their community, and thus Memphis had remained a city without bombings or cross-burnings. "In few cities have the police been so largely and so favorably identified with the civil rights advance," the report continued. "Public order has been maintained in Memphis."[16] Police Commissioner Claude A. Armour was even applauded by a bi-racial recognition dinner. Black leaders agreed that Armour had been fair, had protected them from racist fanatics, and had even helped to desegregate the restaurants. Racial progress was admitted by blacks as well as whites in 1964, the year that a black Memphian, A. W. Willis, Jr., finally won election to the state legislature.

The triumph over segregation in public accommodations produced only temporary satisfaction among blacks. By the end of 1965, blacks in Memphis and elsewhere complained that all the civil rights had done little to eliminate poverty and prejudice or to improve the condition of the masses. A young black attorney, Walter Bailey, complained:

15. Frank Ahlgren to Wallace Witmer, July 24, 1963; Lester A. Rosen, "Speech before Catholic Convention on Religion and Race in the South," March 1965; Maxine Smith to Meeman, Feb. 5, 1964, Meeman Papers.
16. Benjamin Muse, *Memphis* (Atlanta, Ga.: Southern Regional Council, 1964).

I have heard repeatedly that Memphis has made a tremendous degree of racial progress. Obviously the merit of these assertions depends on one's point of view.

Sure, we see "a" Negro working in a department store as a clerk, in an office building, and in non-decision-making administrative jobs. I concede that Negro leaders enjoy some rapport with white leaders and deal with each other as plenipotentiaries. But is this actual progress of any significant degree in terms of changing the racial status quo?[17]

Walter Bailey believed that civil rights had achieved mere tokenism that left most whites committed to the perpetuation of two separate communities, dual school systems, and underemployment for most blacks. The MCCR employment committee had sprinkled a few white-collar blacks in most local businesses but neither the committee, nor Executive Order 11246 prohibiting discrimination by federal contractors, nor Title VII of the Civil Rights Act of 1964, which prohibited discrimination by private firms with more than 100 employees, had secured equal job opportunities for blacks. Blacks held less than 2 percent of the white collar jobs even in firms that held federal contracts. Certainly the large industrial firms such as General Electric's lamp plant in Memphis, which held government contracts, had desegregated restrooms, water fountains, and eating areas, and changed its policy from hiring no blacks in 1961 to employing blacks as one-fourth of their work force by the late sixties. Federal contractors were hiring blacks but they had not given the race 40 percent of the positions, the percentage to which blacks believed they were entitled on the basis of population.[18]

White MCCR members were sympathetic with employers' arguments that their firms could not hire more rapidly than places became available. Surely the companies were not expected to fire whites to make job openings for blacks. Lack of qualified black applicants was also a defense used by employers and generally accepted by white MCCR members. Black Memphians had a median education of less than eight years, while whites had eleven and a

17. *Memphis Press-Scimitar,* Dec. 20, 1965.

18. U.S. Commission on Civil Rights, *Employment, Administration of Justice & Health Services in Memphis-Shelby County, Tenn.* (Washington: GPO, 1967), 3–23; Theodore V. Purcell and Gerald F. Cavanaugh, *Blacks in the Industrial World* (New York: Free Press, 1972), 174–220.

138

half. The gap was even larger if achievement exams were considered; they revealed that black eighth graders tested two grades behind white eighth graders.[19] The differences in average educational achievement generally persuaded white MCCR members to allow companies more time to find qualified white-collar applicants. But the whites admitted that the tactic could be one of delay.

Consider the example of the beer distributors. No company ever stated to the MCCR that it would not hire a black route salesman, but all officials offered excuses, saying that they had no positions and no qualified black applicants. The half-dozen beer distributors in Memphis had been first approached in 1963. Two years later they had done nothing to eliminate racial discrimination in employment. In the fall of 1965 Reverend Samuel Kyles' NAACP employment committee prepared to boycott one of the firms, D. Canale and Company. The threatened boycott produced negotiations with Arthur McCain's MCCR employment committee and finally led to an agreement. Beer distributors were the most difficult industry the MCCR ever attempted to integrate, but black salesmen were finally hired.[20]

While whites applauded each small success, black leaders seemed more indignant that perfect equality still eluded them. The AFL building trade unions refused to desegregate at all. Gerber's Department Store delayed hiring black saleswomen. Other stores and banks continued only token hiring. The public schools continued token integration and refused to hire blacks as top administrators. The city government hired blacks only in 8 percent of the customary white jobs. Blacks were frustrated, and NAACP President Jesse Turner observed, "The promises of hope for a better day remain empty: Negroes have been told to register and vote; to get better education; to love their enemies; to remain loyal. They have done all of these things: yet, their conditions have not improved, noticeably."[21]

Police brutality emerged as a pressing concern for black leaders

19. F. Ray Marshall and Arvil Van Adams, "Negro Employment in Memphis," *Industrial Relations: A Journal of Economy and Society* 9 (May, 1970), 308-23.

20. Jesse H. Turner to A. S. Barboro, May 27, 1965; McCain notes on beer distributors, McCain Papers.

21. Jesse H. Turner, "Annual Statement of President," Memphis *NAACP Reports* (1967), McCain Papers.

now that fear of white violence against civil rights leaders had di-minished in Memphis. Police had always been guilty of occasional brutality, but the black community no longer intended to tolerate excessive force or prejudicial behavior. All talk of good relations between black leaders and the police commissioner had ended by 1966. "Relations between the police and the Negro community are in a sad state of disrepair," the Commission on Civil Rights ob-served. "Only prompt, bold, and decisive leadership on the part of the highest officials of the city and county can avert the disaster which may coincide with the next incident."[22] To negotiate and rem-edy the friction, MCCR created a new committee on disorders and persuaded Commissioner Armour to integrate police squad cars, promote five officers to lieutenants, and end the use of the term "nigger" on the police radio. But Armour rejected a civilian review board and the bi-racial MCCR itself could reach neither an agree-ment nor a solution for police brutality.[23]

In the spring of 1967 the first black leader withdrew from MCCR. Dr. Vasco Smith had grown frustrated with the group's failure to remedy police brutality. In an angry letter he denounced the MCCR as only a fire department concerned with preserving the "precious peace and tranquillity of the business community." He no longer had any use for a group whose only purpose was to put out racial fires. "Since I'm more proficient at building fires than I am at put-ting them out," he said, "I feel out of place on this committee."[24]

Vasco Smith reflected black disillusionment with negotiation, bi-racial committees, and coalition politics. From his wife, Maxine Smith, the executive secretary of the NAACP, he learned about all the instances of brutality, failure to achieve meaningful integration, and failure to achieve equality of opportunity. NAACP President Jesse Turner shared that disillusionment and declared that injus-tices were "not corrected by meek requests but by firm and forceful

22. U.S. Commission on Civil Rights, *Employment, Administration of Justice & Health Services in Memphis-Shelby County, Tenn.,* 52.
23. Burch to MCCR Members, Oct. 10, 1966; Minutes of Executive Committee, Oct. 11, 1966, McCain Papers; *Commercial Appeal,* Oct. 13, 1966.
24. Vasco A. Smith, Jr. to Orgill, April 2, 1967, Orgill Papers.

demands, accompanied by spectacular and aggressive actions."[25] In the municipal election of 1967, black leaders decided not to cooperate with white liberals such as Lucius Burch, who were pushing liberal commissioner Hunter Lane, Jr., for mayor. Instead, they ran their own black, A. W. Willis, Jr., on a platform calling for a civilian review board, open housing, an official Memphis human relations council to replace the MCCR, and revised testing procedures to insure that blacks could qualify for muricipal positions.

In the election of 1967 the black leadership proved to be out of touch with the masses who had remained loyal to Mayor William B. Ingram. The NAACP leadership detested Ingram as completely as the white establishment did because he refused to work with either group. The organization pointed out that despite Ingram's rhetoric for blacks, he had done no more than provide a few Jim Crow jobs. While blacks held 37 percent of the municipal jobs, these were mainly the lowest positions, such as garbage collection; blacks filled no more than 8 percent of the positions traditionally occupied by whites. Although Mayor Ingram caught the wrath of the NAACP, the black citizenry and their pastors still responded favorably to the mayor. They believed that they had too few votes to elect a man of their own race, and they were certain that Ingram should be supported against segregationist Henry Loeb, who was seeking to return to office. When Mayor Ingram's people began a rumor a few days before the election that Willis had been paid by Loeb to enter the campaign and defeat Ingram in the black community, Negroes widely believed the story.[26]

On election day the community split badly. Mayor Ingram decisively beat Willis in the black precincts, winning 53 percent of the black vote, with Willis winning 39 percent and the white liberal Hunter Lane taking only 3 percent. Mayor Ingram made the runoff election only to be defeated by Henry Loeb and a solid white vote. The elections were a disaster for the NAACP leadership in every way

25. Turner, "Annual Statement of President," Memphis *NAACP Reports* (1967).
26. Turner, "Analysis of City Election," *NAACP Reports* (1967); *Commercial Appeal,* Oct. 7, 1967; *Memphis Press-Scimitar,* Oct. 6, 1967.

except that three blacks were elected to the new council and the new mayor, Loeb, offered a negative means of uniting the black community for confrontation politics.[27]

Black leaders had hastened racial polarization when they deserted the old bi-racial coalition of Orgill, Burch, and Lane and promoted a black mayor. The protest leaders believed that the divergence of black and white interests required an end to coalition and compromise. The politics of moderation was now replaced by the politics of race. But black leaders were not alone in deserting the moderates. In the white community, as we shall see, a white separatist movement also recognized the divergence of ethnic interests, rejected the old Democratic liberals and promoted a white Republicanism to defeat the new black democracy.

27. The black councilmen were Fred Davis, Reverend James Netters, and J.O. Patterson, Jr.

8.

The Emergence of White Republicanism

White resistance to black pressure for social change elevated the Republican party to political dominance in Shelby County. Memphians alarmed by integration sit-ins, protest marches, civil rights legislation, and urban riots expressed their fears and resentment by voting for the party that offered most resistance to black demands. Republicanism may have reflected a more sophisticated style than the old-fashioned Southern racism, but the party's polite urban opposition to civil rights certainly provided Memphians with a political opportunity to say no to the Negro revolution.

The emergence of Republicanism as the local party of white resistance marked a surprising shift in the tradition of a political organization which had long been the party of black Memphians. Ever since the Civil War, the local Republican party had been shunned by Memphis whites except those who wanted post office jobs or those few Northern Republicans who had moved into the city. Not only the party membership but also the local leadership came under black domination. Robert R. Church, Jr., son of Memphis's first wealthy black capitalist, established his control over the local party before World War I and controlled the federal patronage until a Democrat —Franklin D. Roosevelt—captured the presidency. Church then gave party control over to Lieutenant George W. Lee, who in turn maintained the local machinery, waiting for the return of national Republican victories that would restore prestige and federal patronage to local black Republicans.[1]

A growing number of white economic conservatives emerged to challenge Lieutenant Lee's party leadership in the 1950s. Southern Democrats who hated Franklin Roosevelt's New Deal, especially the cotton merchants on Front Street, began to vote Republican. Although Roosevelt's Agricultural Adjustment Administration had given cotton farmers higher prices, the federal program priced American cotton out of the world market and drastically cut back on cotton acreage. These policies reduced the volume of cotton business and turned Memphis's cotton market into a depressed and declining industry. When President Harry S Truman continued federal controls and federal welfare into the fifties, lifelong Democrats such as Everett R. Cook, head of one of the three largest cotton companies in the world, grew alarmed about "creeping socialism." Cook joined other white conservatives who did not wish to work with Lieutenant Lee and organized the Citizens for Eisenhower. They hoped that a Republican victory would restore free enterprise and decentralized government.[2]

Dwight Eisenhower came nearer to winning Shelby County in 1952 than any other Republican in history, and four years later he did win a majority. Memphis whites became Eisenhower Republicans in national presidential elections, but their support was more for the president than for his party. They continued as Democrats in state and local politics. They avoided Republican primaries and allowed Lieutenant Lee to continue his control over the local Republican party. Young white attorneys such as Lewis Donelson III, Alexander Dann, and Leo Buchignani, sought repeatedly to wrest control from Lieutenant Lee, but not until the presidency of John F. Kennedy and the beginning of local integration did whites turn to the Republican party primary in sufficient numbers for the attor-

1. Tucker, *Lieutenant Lee of Beale Street,* 68–155; Church, *The Robert R. Churches of Memphis,* 87–148.
2. *Commercial Appeal,* Feb. 1, 1952; *Memphis Press-Scimitar,* Oct. 8, 1952.

neys to depose the old black boss, Lieutenant Lee, from the party's state executive committee.[3]

The early sixties produced a political revolution in Memphis as blacks deserted the Republican party while a mass of whites moved in to take over. To be sure, black desertion of the Republican party had begun during the thirties when Roosevelt's welfare policies appealed to the black community. By the forties Memphis blacks regularly voted Democratic, but black Republicanism also persisted, and as late as 1956 Lieutenant Lee secured a majority for Eisenhower in the local black precincts. But in 1960 Lee's Republican leadership failed completely when blacks voted two-to-one for John F. Kennedy. Blacks deserted Lee to follow the younger civil rights leaders in Memphis who had recommended Democrats because of their stronger civil rights program and their promise of a $1.25 minimum wage.[4]

While blacks began to view Democrats as the party of civil rights, whites began to see Republicans as the party for white Southerners. The president of the local Young Republicans, Ira Lipman, advertised in 1960 that his party no longer stood for civil rights. "Our big job," Lipman said, "is to convince the thousands of voters who are conservative that the Republican party of today is not the radical party of Reconstruction days—that ours is the party with the principles they really believe in: the importance of the individual and free enterprise."[5]

Whites gave Richard Nixon a Shelby County majority in 1960, but they would later be even more enthusiastic about Senator Barry Goldwater, who analyzed the reasons for Nixon's narrow defeat in the electoral college and concluded that Republicans had erred in promising any federal support for the civil rights of black Americans. Republicans had lost the presidency in the South, Goldwater said, because they had been reluctant to pay the market price for white votes in the Deep South. As a presidential hopeful, Goldwater began to solicit the Southern segregationist vote, promising to "bend every muscle" to uphold state control of education and with-

3. *Commercial Appeal,* Nov. 6, 1952, Nov. 7, 1956; *Memphis Press-Scimitar,* Aug. 3, 1962.
4. *Commercial Appeal,* Nov. 9, 1960; *Tri-State Defender,* Nov. 19, 1960.
5. *Memphis Press-Scimitar,* Oct. 22, 1960.

draw the GOP's support of integration in the public schools. Goldwater willingly became the segregationist candidate and thus the great favorite of whites in Memphis and the Deep South.[6]

Goldwaterism in Memphis had intimate connections with the rightwing extremism that spread across the South in the early sixties, thriving on fears that the Soviet Union had achieved a missile superiority over America and that here at home Communists disguised as liberals were undermining the country by pushing racial integration and social welfare legislation. All the extremist groups— the Christian Anti-Communist Crusade, the John Birch Society, the Minute Men—knew that Chief Justice Earl Warren had to be a card-carrying Communist or a dupe of the Communists. The academic capital of these ultraconservative groups, little Harding College, had been creating propaganda at Searcy, Arkansas for more than a decade. It spent $200,000 a year on audiovisual materials to persuade Americans that liberalism equaled socialism and socialism equaled Communism—therefore, our greatest danger came from the liberals at home who had taken over the schools and colleges. With funds obtained from rightwing capitalists, Harding College produced expensive technicolor films such as "Communism on the Map," a dramatized lecture in which the whole world is shown turning red or pink. Even France, Sweden, and Norway were said to be in the Communist camp for all practical purposes. "Communism on the Map" became the great favorite of the John Birch Society and all other rightwing groups. Locally, the Memphis American Legion raised $10,000 to finance a sustained showing of the film throughout the Mid-South and to distribute copies of J. Edgar Hoover's *Masters of Deceit* in every public school.[7]

One Memphian attracted to the anti-Communist crusade was Robert James, an Iowa-born Republican, who had moved to Mem-

6. *New York Times,* Nov. 19, 1961; Tucker, *Lieutenant Lee of Beale Street,* 179-99.

7. Donald Janson and Bernard Eismann, *The Far Right* (New York: McGraw-Hill, 1963), 92-100; Betty E. Chmaj, "Paranoid Patriotism: The Radical Right and the South," *Atlantic Monthly* 210 (Nov. 1962), 91-93; Philip Horton, "Revivalism on the Far Right," *The Reporter* 25 (July 20, 1961), 25; "Thunder on the Right," *Newsweek* 58 (Dec. 4, 1961), 18-30; Fred W. Lucas to Orgill, Feb. 27, 1961, Orgill Papers.

phis in the thirties with Firestone Tire and Rubber Company. James had gone into business for himself, selling a sweeping and cleaning service for offices and industries. Over the years he continued to operate his Memphis Housecleaning Company and taught Methodist Sunday school until fear of liberalism and socialism pushed him into politics. James attended the chamber of commerce seminars on politics and joined the Citizens Association. While viewing "Communism on the Map" at the Lions Club he became so alarmed that he immediately volunteered to head the crusade against Communism of the local American Legion. He showed the film more than three hundred times in churches, clubs, and schools across the Mid-South. In recognition of James's industrious anti-Communism, J. Edgar Hoover presented him with the highest award from the Freedom Foundation of Valley Forge.[8]

Because of James's anti-Communist leadership, local Republicans asked him to run for Congress in 1962. Memphis Republican leaders were by no means all rightwing extremists; they did hate Communism, liberalism, and the New Deal, but 20 percent of them were willing to accept federally-imposed integration.[9] Those Republicans who called on James were led by Lewis Donelson III, a local tax attorney, who had participated in all the civic reform organizations including the interracial MCCR. He had headed the committee that desegregated downtown department stores. Donelson was never an extremist who believed Dr. Martin Luther King, Jr., to be a Communist, but apparently he and other moderate Republican leaders viewed James as an attractive candidate whose conservatism would appeal to white Memphians—and they were right.

Bob James announced his candidacy in 1962 against Crump's representative, Cliff Davis, who had held the position since 1940. The elderly, heavy-drinking congressman was certainly conservative, but he was also lethargic, and Bob James charged that Davis

8. Robert James interview, Sanitation Strike Archives; *Memphis Press-Scimitar,* March 24, May 3, 1962.

9. A statistical study of 250 members of the local Republican Association is found in an excellent honors thesis, see Paul M. Ruden, "Transitional Politics: The Development of a Two-Party System in Memphis and Shelby County, Tennessee" (senior honors thesis, Yale Univ., 1964).

had not vigorously defended the country against Communism from abroad or socialism at home. "The House of Representatives is the only hope," James said, "for those citizens who would head off the deadly drift towards a fatal plunge into the cataracts of socialistic government." He sought to persuade Memphians that Representative Davis had been a Kennedy Democrat—soft on Communism and socialism. A favorite election handout was the bar of soap with which James dramatized his campaign to "clean Davis out of Congress." The soap carried the message: "A vote for Bob James for Congress is a vote against rubber-stamping the Socialist soft soap of the far-out New Frontier." James talked chiefly of economic policy and foreign policy. He said little about race except to condemn the federal intervention that forcefully integrated nearby University of Mississippi in the fall of 1962. He did not have to say much about race because everybody knew where he stood. He had led the move to strip Lieutenant Lee, and therefore the black community, of any position in the Republican party. By merely labeling himself a conservative, James made his racial position clear: a conservative was then understood to be a segregationist. On election day he did win a majority of the white vote but lost by 1,200 votes because blacks voted heavily against him.[10]

If Bob James truly reflected local party attitudes, the heart of Memphis Republicans stood somewhere between conservative and extremist, definitely opposed to social welfare liberalism and to civil rights for blacks, but stopping short of radical rightism. James had attended a few John Birch Society meetings and subscribed to their magazine but did not join the group, not because he disagreed with them, he said, but because the organization seemed a less effective advocate of anti-Communism than his own American Legion. James did work with a local leader of the Birch Society, industrialist C. Arthur Bruce, to denounce the proposed Civil Rights Bill of 1964 and to call for contributions to organize a campaign against the legislation.[11] None of this fraternization with the Right offended Republicans, who in 1964 again made James their congressional candi-

10. *Memphis Press-Scimitar,* May 16, Oct. 9, 15, Nov. 3, 7, 1962.
11. C. Arthur Bruce, Martin J. Condon III, R. B. James et al. to Taylor Hayes, Jan. 14, 1964, George W. Lee Papers, Amistad Research Center, Dillard University;

date, chairman of their local party, and a Goldwater delegate to the Republican National Convention.

The Memphis congressional campaign of 1964 presented a classic contest between liberals and conservatives. Representative Cliff Davis had been deposed in the Democratic primary by George Grider, the liberal civic reformer from Lucius Burch's law office and Edmund Orgill's political campaigns. Grider believed in both integration and social welfare liberalism. He fully endorsed President Lyndon Johnson's Great Society programs. Bob James voiced the conservative opposition by firmly opposing all the federal programs, especially Medicare and the War on Poverty. He proclaimed the word "no" to be the sweetest sound in the English language. "We say no many times," James declared, "no to riots in the streets, no to trespassing on private property in the name of Civil Rights, no to filth and indecency wherever we find it. . . ."[12]

White Memphians voted more than two to one for Bob James and Barry Goldwater in the 1964 election. Even the blue-collar precincts, such as Frayser, rejected Lyndon Johnson and George Grider. But the Democrats still won in Memphis because blacks cast 99 percent of their votes against the Republicans and Goldwaterism. The white outrage in Memphis at being outvoted was expressed by Bob James who lamented: "the respectable people have been outvoted." He calculated that more than 70 percent of whites had voted for him and Goldwater, with only labor, the aged, Jews, and Negroes opposing.[13]

The racial nature of the new Republicanism had been widely publicized in Memphis by the local black politician, Lieutenant George W. Lee. After being voted off the state Republican executive committee in 1962, Lee continued to fight for a delegate position to the Republican National Convention in 1964. He carried his unsuccessful campaign all the way to a nationally televised protest before the

---

Robert James television interview, Oct. 4, 1964, George Grider Papers, Mississippi Valley Collection.

12. James, television interview, Oct. 4, 1964, Grider Papers; for Grider's military record see George Grider and Lydel Sims, *War Fish* (Boston: Little, Brown, 1958).

13. Commercial Appeal, Nov. 4, 5, 1964; Michael Lupfer, "A Correlational Analysis of the Grider-James Election," Grider Papers.

credentials committee of the San Francisco convention. He charged that the radical right had taken over the Memphis party and turned it into a lily-white group appealing to racism and hatred. The Goldwater convention rejected Lee's appeal, to be sure, but he had achieved wide publicity and returned to Memphis declaring that every black Memphian had an obligation to vote against Bob James and Barry Goldwater, candidates whom Lee considered to be right-wing extremists.[14]

The Republican party had clearly attracted the vast majority of white Memphians and Southern segregationists with its anti-black image. Goldwater carried only Arizona and five states in the Deep South. The decisive sectional attraction of Goldwaterism was obvious. Southern whites living in counties with a large black population voted overwhelmingly for Goldwater. Whites living in largely white communities were more fearful of Goldwater's extremist stands on social security, TVA, or Vietnam. Memphis whites reflected the general trend in the Deep South when they deserted the Democratic party and left it to the control of black Democrats.[15]

Democrats lost the next congressional election in Memphis. Only the extremely polarizing Goldwater campaign had been able to bring out 65 percent of the registered black voters, enough to override the white Republican vote. In the next election, less than 50 percent of the blacks turned out, but almost 70 percent of the whites voted to turn George Grider out of office. Bob James did not have the pleasure of winning in 1966, but a fellow Goldwaterite, Dan Kuykendall, achieved the victory. A conservative soap salesman from Texas, he had been transferred to Memphis in 1955 as general manager of the local manufacturing plant of Procter and Gamble. He first ran for office in 1964, winning 46 percent of the Tennessee vote in his unsuccessful Goldwaterite campaign against Senator Albert Gore. Kuykendall hated liberalism, civil rights, and Communism just as passionately as Bob James. In 1966 he accused Congressman Grider of supporting open housing, Medicare, poverty programs,

14. Tucker, *Lieutenant Lee of Beale Street,* 184–98.
15. Albert Gore, *Let the Glory Out: My South and Its Politics* (New York: Viking, 1972), 183; William C. Havard (ed.) *The Changing Politics of the South* (Baton Rouge: Louisiana State Univ. Press, 1972), 336–37.

and Johnson's no-win Vietnam war. Since both candidates favored escalating the war with Vietnam, this issue had little to do with the outcome of the election. More decisive was the white resentment of George Grider, a belief that he had pushed only pro-black legislation in Congress. Grider's small white support declined, while black apathy permitted even more of his Negro vote to vanish. The Democratic civic reformers had lost their influence in local elections, and conservative Dan Kuykendall would represent Memphis.[16]

The Kuykendall victory began an era of Republican supremacy in Shelby County. So few whites would vote Democratic that Republicans never failed to outvote the Democratic blacks who counted 40 percent of the local population. White Democrats were eliminated from local government. The city council elected in 1967, for example, contained not one white Democrat. Only the three black councilmen, who represented black districts, claimed to be Democrats; the whites labeled themselves either Republicans or independents.[17] Successful white Democrats became an extinct species in Memphis now that the white community had moved into the Republican party. The racial polarization into separate parties reflected a greater racial antagonism in local government. The civil rights movement had gone far enough to threaten the vast majority of white Memphians who voted Republican, and they no longer tolerated politicians who compromised with blacks. They demanded toughness. Racial confrontation was almost inevitable now that whites had united in resistance while blacks had grown impatient and united in pressing for more dramatic change.

16. Grider-Kuykendall debate, Sept. 25, 1966; Grider to Burch, Nov. 10, 1966, Grider Papers; *Memphis Press-Scimitar,* Oct. 27, 1966; *Commercial Appeal,* Nov. 9, 10, 1966; Dan Kuykendall interview, Sanitation Strike Archives; Ralph Nader Congress Project, *Dan Kuykendall* (New York: Grossman, 1972).

17. *Memphis Press-Scimitar,* Nov. 3, 1967.

9.

The Garbage Strike

"Carrying the Man's garbage" paid so little in status or wages that black Memphians gladly left the work to sharecroppers who migrated in from nearby rural communities. The typical "barn" or administrative subunit of the sanitation department hired almost exclusively from the same agricultural county. Sometime in the past a black from rural Fayette County, Tennessee (adjoining Shelby County on the east) had secured work as a garbage man and carried news of job openings at his barn to friends and relatives back in his home county, where laborers had become obsolete as the planters turned to mechanical cotton-pickers and chemical herbicides. White supervisors in the Memphis Sanitation Department willingly hired Fayette County blacks because these "country boys" were docile and industrious as well as available. Thus most barns in Memphis came to employ almost exclusively workers from Fayette County.[1]

Rural blacks seemed unlikely candidates for unionization, but during the sixties such municipal workers were aggressively recruited by the American Federation of State, County, and Municipal Employees, which became the fastest growing union in America. One

1. Thomas W. Collins, "Unionization in a Secondary Labor Market," *Human Organization* 36 (Summer 1977), 141.

of the few city-born garbage collectors in Memphis, T.O. Jones, had long been working to unionize fellow workers in the AFSCME. A short, round, determined man, Jones had learned unionization as a shipyard worker on the West Coast before the 1958 recession forced him back home to Memphis, where he accepted a job in the city sanitation department. Jones quietly began organizing his fellow workers, an agonizingly slow process that continued for almost a decade. Even though he and more than thirty of his union converts were fired in 1963 for attempting to call a strike, the little man kept at his self-appointed mission and went on the AFSCME payroll as a union organizer in 1964. In 1966, after failing again in a strike attempt, T.O. Jones waited impatiently for an incident that would finally persuade most of the 1,300 sanitation workers to walk out and enforce his demand for official union recognition by the city. The incident finally happened in February, 1968, when twenty-two men working on sewers and drains were arbitrarily sent home by the sanitation department on a rainy day no worse than other recent days during which they had been permitted to work. White supervisors would, of course, draw wages for the entire day, while black laborers were to receive pay for only two hours. The grievance could have been settled by pay for half a day, which T.O. Jones sought to win for the men, but on payday the twenty-two men received wages for only two hours. This minor labor grievance and the accidental death of two men crushed in a garbage compressor created sufficient emotional anger for T.O. Jones to call a strike meeting on Sunday night.[2]

Fewer than forty sanitation workers had been paying dues in AFSCME Local 1733, but more than 400 turned out for the meeting in Labor Temple on South Second. Jones reminded the assembled men that the two Memphis widows had received no insurance benefits when their husbands were crushed in the garbage compressors. Memphis garbage men earned less than $70 a week, while New York sanitation men, following their recent strike, received $160. During rainy weeks, local black workers received far less than $70. So the indignant workers were persuaded to issue demands to the Memphis Sanitation Department. With the meeting still in progress, T.O.

2. T.O. Jones interview, Sanitation Strike Archives.

Jones rushed off to make immediate demands known to the administrative head of the sanitation department. The demands were rejected, to be sure, and Jones returned to tell his men that the city offered them nothing. Angry garbage men resolved to withhold their labor, and the next morning fewer than 200 of the 1,300 sanitation workers went to work—a successful Monday morning wildcat strike as surprising to the national AFSCME as it was to the Memphis city government.[3]

Mayor Henry Loeb reacted with a tough, uncompromising stance. The inflexible mayor declared the strike against Memphis to be illegal under state law, and he insisted that it must be immediately ended. When the workers refused to return to their jobs, replacement hiring began. Mayor Loeb did consent to talk with national leaders of the AFSCME who came to negotiate for T. O Jones's men, but he never shifted from his position that the strike was illegal and Memphis would never recognize a union for the sanitation workers. The mayor was six feet five inches tall, and he delighted in expressing himself in a cowboy code: "I don't make deals." He never doubted that he would quickly break the municipal strike and win the overwhelming applause of white Memphians who had elected him.[4]

The strike might easily have been snuffed out if the labor dispute had not quickly turned into a civil rights struggle. Black civil rights leaders were eager to embarrass the segregationist mayor and rallied quickly to the side of the garbage workers. The local NAACP held a press conference, on Friday, to announce that the protest organization would join the union picket lines. "We are moving in to unite the community behind the garbage men," Reverend Samuel B. Kyles and Mrs. Maxine Smith announced for their organization. NAACP leaders and middle-class black pastors joined in the protest marches downtown and suffered from the police department's indiscriminate use of the chemical Mace, which made them even more committed to defeating the city administration. On February 23,

3. Joan Beifuss, "The Memphis Garbage Strike" (a massive book manuscript that was sponsored by the Memphis Search for Meaning Committee, which Mrs. Beifuss generously permitted me to read).
4. David Caywood interview, Sanitation Strike Archives; Gerold Frank, *An American Death* (Garden City: Doubleday, 1972), 11-2.

when a police car crowded a line of protesting sanitation workers, strikers grabbed the bumper and rocked the car. Police officers jumped out and turned their spray cans on every black in sight, innocent bystanders, ministers, and garbage collectors alike; and in so doing they converted moderates into radicals.[5]

Angry clergymen called an emergency meeting of the Interdenominational Ministers Alliance, the one organization which included all Negro denominations. The sixty ministers who met in Mason Temple included both elderly, many of whom had been moderates at one time, and angry young militants, but they joined together in voting to pressure the white establishment by calling an economic boycott. The targets, downtown stores and the two daily Scripps-Howard newspapers, were announced on Sunday morning from the pulpit of most of the city's black churches. Some pastors even used their sermons to compare the strikers with the Old Testament prophets who crusaded against injustice, took up special collections for the workers, and asked their congregations to join them in daily marches to downtown Memphis. In the days that followed, active ministers and NAACP officers led long processions down Main Street during business hours to dramatize and strengthen the boycott. Workers, ministers, and community people filled nightly prayer meetings in the churches to capacity and in less than a week raised $15,000 for the strikers. Downtown sales dropped by 35 percent as the black community united firmly behind the garbage strike.[6]

Strike rhetoric increased sharply in the protest meetings. Former moderates, such as the Reverend H. Ralph Jackson, had turned militant after their painful and unnecessary macing. The angry Reverend Jackson publicly toyed with the possibility of violence, encouraging the local black power group, the Invaders, to announce their solution—armed resistance—to strike supporters. When an elderly accommodationist pastor, Dr. W. Herbert Brewster, admonished those who would use force ("Don't reduce yourself so low that you will hate any man"), Jackson ridiculed this Christian doctrine of

5. *Memphis Press-Scimitar,* Feb. 16, 24, 1968; Jim Bishop, *The Days of Martin Luther King Jr.* (New York: Putnam's, 1971), 488.
6. *Wall Street Journal,* March 8, 1968; Memphis *Commercial Appeal,* Feb. 25, March 3, 1968; *Tri-State Defender,* March 2, 1968.

love. "He didn't get a whiff of that gas, did he," Jackson told the strike crowd. "Dr. Brewster better go back and pray some more, because he hasn't got me liking Loeb yet. . . ." The audience roared with delight. "You better be careful, Doctor," Jackson further warned Brewster. "You might be calling for water while the rest of us are calling for fire." To dramatize the point, Reverend Jackson pulled out a gold-plated cigar lighter and held it high.[7]

Because Mayor Loeb secured a court injunction prohibiting union officials from participating in strike activities, the clergy began to direct the action and voice the strikers' demands. Their Sunday sermons, pep talks, and protests before the city council all carried the same message: race was the key issue in the strike and violence was almost certain if the strikers did not win at least partial victory. In fact, violence had already surfaced during the dispute in the form of isolated but ominous incidents of fire bombings, bottle throwing, and trash fires, which were reported almost nightly.[8]

The old Memphis Committee on Community Relations did recommend a compromise to end the growing racial hostility. MCCR Chairman Edmund Orgill and Vice-chairman Frank Ahlgren supported a statement drafted by a young attorney, David Caywood (Lucius Burch's son-in-law), that contained both Loeb's expressed principles on the labor dispute ("illegal, immoral strike") and all of the union's essential demands. After an MCCR strategy meeting, Caywood and Ned Cook, president of Cook Industries Inc. and one of Loeb's personal friends, carried the strike solution to the mayor. But the MCCR compromise was adamantly rejected. Henry Loeb had been elected, he said, to be the garbage men's "keeper," and he would never abandon his "moral obligation" to protect them from "this evil union." After their compromise was rejected, the MCCR abandoned any hope of influence and retired quietly to the sidelines.[9]

The black pastors and NAACP officials brought in prominent civil rights leaders who could give the Memphis strike a national image.

7. J. Edwin Stanfield, *In Memphis: More than a Garbage Strike* (Atlanta, Ga.: Southern Regional Council, 1968), 42–44.
8. *Wall Street Journal,* March 8, 1968; *Commercial Appeal,* March 12, 1968.
9. David Caywood to Frank Ahlgren, March 5, 1968; Caywood interview, John Spence interview, Frank Ahlgren interview, Sanitation Strike Archives.

After all, Reverend James Lawson said, "this is a significant turn in the civil rights movement and a new chapter in labor history. Never before has a union been backed by a whole community like this." Jesse Turner, a local black banker and board member of the national NAACP, flew to New York and brought back the organization's executive secretary, Roy Wilkins, to speak to a huge rally of 9,000 on the evening of March 14. On March 18 Martin Luther King, Jr. came and spoke to an even larger rally. The spirit of the crowd, which was more enthusiastic than any other King had seen in recent months, led him to commit himself more to their struggle than he had at first intended. King declared that black Memphians ought to have a one-day general strike, and the audience went wild. "You arrange a march for that day," he shouted, "and I'll come back to Memphis to lead it."[10]

"Friday!" they shouted.

"Friday!" he agreed. But by Friday sixteen inches of snow blocked the streets, and the event was rescheduled for March 28.

The coming of King alarmed the Memphis City Council, provoking a legislative effort to override Mayor Loeb's refusal to settle with the AFSCME. Initially, the three black councilmen—Fred Davis, James Netters, and J. O. Patterson, Jr.—had been alone in their willingness to accept the union's demand that dues payments be deducted automatically from paychecks, but by early March they were joined by Jerred Blanchard, a Missouri-born banker's son who had gone to Yale on an athletic scholarship. The large, jovial Republican attorney was a man of compassion and Christian conscience who had been assured by Republican businessmen at his Memphis Country Club, "Oh, the check-off, that's not too bad. If that's all you gotta give 'em, give it to 'em." So Blanchard made a plea that his fellow councilmen take the initiative and settle the strike. He asked:

> Well, is it worth a life? Is this check-off that they want worth a life, because I've got a notion that before this thing is over somebody is

10. Bishop, *The Days of Martin Luther King Jr.,* 493; *Commercial Appeal,* March 15, 19, 1968; *New York Times,* March 18, 1968.

gonna get killed. And then we're gonna have to say yes, denying them a check-off was worth a human life. And I, for one, just can't say this.[11]

Most white councilmen regarded Blanchard's change of position as contemptible. They were certain that serious violence would never occur in Memphis and that by deserting the mayor, Blanchard had foolishly turned cowardly and appeasing. So the councilman felt that he was now regarded as the "fourth nigger on the council."

The white council majority accurately reflected the conservatism and anti-black sentiment of Memphis suburbia. Tom Todd, a member of the Memphis Cotton Exchange, was rigidly anti-black. The Virginia-born conservative was a model of manners and politeness as well as the cotton planter's reluctance to accept any possibility of racial equality or unionization. Businessmen Robert James and W. T. McAdams were less anti-black than Todd but still inclined to believe that Martin Luther King, Jr. was a Communist and that all appeasement of black unionism was immoral. Councilmen Wyeth Chandler, Billy Hyman, Philip Perel, and Gwen Awsumb were more moderate on race but so economically conservative and anti-union that they would never vote to override Mayor Loeb's opposition to compromise.[12]

Only two other white councilmen—Lewis Donelson III and Downing Pryor—joined Blanchard and the blacks, making the vote six to seven, one short of a majority for overruling Loeb. Donelson became the most articulate and vocal critic of Loeb's refusal to accept dues check-off. Representing intelligent conservatism—the awareness that racial harmony should be regarded as more important than blocking the growth of municipal unionism—Donelson had been frightened by the announcement that King would come to Memphis. Violence generally erupted during campaigns led by the civil rights leader, and certainly racial tension always increased in cities targeted for nonviolent confrontation demonstrations. To prevent increasing racial strife, Donelson worked to build a majority against the mayor, persuading council chairman Downing Pryor to

11. Jerred Blanchard interview, Sanitation Strike Archives.
12. Lewis Donelson III interview, Robert James interview, W. T. McAdams interview, Sanitation Strike Archives.

act with him but failing to persuade Gwen Awsumb that she too should vote for a dues check-off. Mrs. Awsumb and the remainder of the council stood firmly with the white Memphis majority, which wanted both the strike and the union broken.[13]

In attempting to reschedule King's march, Negro ministers were disturbed by the local black power group, the Invaders, who argued that if the demonstrations were to have any effect, then violence was absolutely necessary. "Man," one Invader said, "if you expect honkies to get the message, you got to break some windows." The churchmen insisted that King's march be peaceful: "you can join the rest of us in a nonviolent march," the ministers said, "or you can boycott it." But when the demonstration began on the morning of March 28, the Invaders were there, mingling among the 5,000 peaceful marchers, equipped with heavy sticks. Beale Street people, shoplifters, and pickpockets who had been unable to practice their trade because of the absence of crowds in the downtown area, were also there, gathered in groups along the sidewalks. They apparently shattered the first store windows as the march approached. Young militants left the line of march on Beale Street to join the window breaking and looting that turned the demonstration into a riot. Police responded with tear gas and force. One black youth was killed, sixty were injured, three hundred were arrested, and King's ability to lead his people in a nonviolent demonstration was now questioned by every white journalist in America.[14]

Many white Memphians rejoiced over the failed demonstration. "Yesterday was a great day for Memphis," Councilmen Tom Todd, Bob James, and Wyeth Chandler agreed. "We showed them that we weren't going to put up with any violence in Memphis." The council leadership remained unwilling to admit that the riot had revealed the city to be a powder keg, even though Lewis Donelson denounced his colleagues for making an "asinine statement" and failing to perceive that the riot would be remembered as a black day, poisoning race relations for the future. Donelson spoke for fewer

13. Donelson interview, Downing Pryor interview, Blanchard interview, Sanitation Strike Archives.
14. Bishop, *The Days of Martin Luther King,* 5–6; *Commercial Appeal,* March 29, 1968.

Memphians than did the president of the local chamber of commerce, Thomas W. Faires, who believed no problem existed except black shiftlessness and activist ministers. "If the Negro ministers would tend to their ministering instead of trying to stir things up," Faires said, "we wouldn't have had this trouble."[15]

While white Memphians remained confident that they were winning the strike, Martin King immediately began planning a new demonstration. Since he was then organizing a poor people's march on Washington, King felt compelled to reestablish his nonviolent reputation in Memphis. He met with representatives of the Invaders, promised to bring them in on the plans, and seemed to have guarantees of a successful and nonviolent demonstration. It was while preparing for a second march in Memphis that King was shot down by an assassin's bullet.[16]

The murder of the nation's leading spokesman for civil rights provoked arson, looting, and sniping in Memphis and across urban America, causing pressures that even Mayor Loeb could no longer resist. The White House and the attorney general called to say that settlement of the labor dispute was in the best national interest of the United States. Prominent members of the local chamber of commerce, who had opposed all compromise with the union, now visited Loeb to insist that he settle the nine-week-old strike.[17] Local white leadership lamented that the assassination had happened in Memphis, where it tarnished the city's image, inviting derisive journalistic descriptions as a "Southern backwater" and a "decaying river town." In an effort to end the racial confrontation and restore the city's reputation, Henry Loeb agreed to settle—to pay the extra ten cents an hour if local philanthropist Abe Plough would provide the money; to permit dues check-off if it was arranged indirectly through a credit union and then paid to the union; and almost to "recognize" the AFSCME by entering a "memorandum of understanding" with them.

15. *New York Times,* March 31, 1968; Donelson interview, Sanitation Strike Archives.
16. David L. Lewis, *King: A Critical Biography* (Baltimore: Penguin, 1970), 383–89; Frank, *An American Death,* 34–113.
17. Ned Cook interview, Sanitation Strike Archives.

The garbage strike ended on April 16 but left the city traumatized and divided. While a few whites were guilt-ridden, more were fearful and angry. Black leadership pushed on for solutions to other grievances such as police brutality and black unemployment. To compensate for the death of Dr. King and to prevent additional violence, blacks argued, the white leadership must move to end all racism and discrimination. Strike leader Reverend Lawson threatened to begin boycotts of local companies that refused to hire more blacks. "We have the troops now," Lawson said, "to move systematically from industry to industry." A SCLC field representative added the threat that Memphis would be made a "martyr city" and forced to "pay a higher price than any other city in the nation for the death of Dr. Martin Luther King Jr."[18]

18. *New York Times,* April 21, 1968; *Memphis Press-Scimitar,* April 26, 1968.

10.

Believe in Memphis

The sanitation strike terminated organized civic reform in Memphis. The Memphis Committee on Community Relations had unsuccessfully recommended a compromise to Mayor Loeb early in the racial confrontation. It then abandoned any hope of influence, quietly disbanding entirely after the strike settlement and giving in to the demand of black leadership that the MCCR be replaced by an official Human Relations Commission appointed by the city and the county governments. Approval of the new Memphis and Shelby County Human Relations Commission on 30 April 1968 marked the final retirement of the old municipal reformers from organized civic leadership. Memphis, after twenty years, no longer had a MCCR, a Citizens Association, or a Civic Research Committee.

Civic reform was a casualty of racial and political polarization, which snapped the ties binding the old coalition against Crump. Relations between the reform Democrats and their Republican allies were embittered after the Republicans' 1966 defeat of Congressman George Grider, making bipartisan reform difficult. Reformers from both parties had cooperated on the POP charter, but after Republicans won political dominance in the 1967 elections to the new city council, they had little interest in continuing their civic reform activity or the old civic organizations. Blacks too had departed from the coalition, except for those old-fashioned moderates such as Le-Moyne College President Hollis Price, who had never succumbed to the new militancy. Black NAACP leadership no longer believed volunteerism to be of any value for ending racism and discrimination; mass action and political pressure were viewed as the only useful tactics. If whites wanted to be helpful, they could support the black demand for "40 percent of Memphis." Black banker and local NAACP president Jesse Turner asserted: "Well, look. We're forty per cent of the population. We want forty per cent of the money, forty per cent of the land, forty per cent of the jobs." This demand offended white liberals, who had been working not for quotas but for equality of opportunity. Lucius Burch, who was Martin Luther King's attorney in Memphis, surely spoke not only for his group but for virtually every white Memphian when he rejected Turner's demand. "Well, you'll have to put a bullet in me to get that done," Burch said. "Unless you're worthy of it you're not going to get forty per cent of anything. You'll get what you're entitled to, on a fair and equitable basis."[1] If even Lucius Burch opposed black demands, then civil rights leaders frankly preferred to forget about white liberals and take their cause to businessmen and the chamber of commerce.

The local chamber seemed an unlikely organization for dealing with black problems even though it had become a leading advocate of other governmental reforms. The chamber had reflected a white racism widespread in Memphis. The executive officer kept almost no information about the black community, and when asked for it was known to turn to his secretary and say, "See what we've got in the nigger file." But the chamber was changing, and the garbage strike certainly accelerated a new interest in race. Now that blacks were regarded as the number one problem in Memphis, some business leaders expected a more enlightened attitude from the chamber. The downtown bankers and the heads of Holiday Inns of America and Plough Incorporated, who jointly contributed more than a million dollars for the national advertising of Memphis, led a reorgani-

1. Ned Cook interview, Jesse Turner interview, Russell Sugarmon interview, Sanitation Strike Archives.

zation of the chamber of commerce that included the hiring of a more enlightened executive director. The new officer, David Cooley, believed good business required dealing with racial problems.[2]

The new leaders of the chamber of commerce had not been civic reformers; they were money-makers who never participated in organizations associated with Orgill. Their primary concern, the economic growth of Memphis and their own profits, had been aroused by a planning commission study. In *The Economy of Metropolitan Memphis* (Memphis, 1965), Hammer, Green, Siler Associates made the tantalizing prediction that metropolitan Memphis could double in size during the next twenty-five years. Such an unprecedented quantum leap, the study concluded, required only that Memphis continue to surpass Nashville, Little Rock, and Birmingham as the urban-industrial service center of the Mid-South. Doubling the size of the city and its banking business appealed strongly to Allen B. Morgan of the First National Bank, Lewis K. McKee of National Bank of Commerce, and W. Porter Grace of Union Planters National Bank. At a November 1967 meeting with nine other business leaders, the bankers agreed to the Greater Memphis Program reorganizing the chamber of commerce and launching a national campaign to advertise Memphis.[3]

The garbage strike and the death of King confounded the Greater Memphis Program, persuading the businessmen that their own black community had become the major obstacle to growth. The leaders now had to persuade those Northern executives who were relocating their plants and home offices that Memphis was making progress toward solving the race problem. When local black leaders demanded action on black unemployment and underemployment, the chamber leaders were forced to provide jobs and to explain the Greater Memphis Program as a campaign to find employment for blacks as well as whites. Blacks were now recruited as chamber members, appointed to leadership positions, and regularly con-

2. Redding S. Sugg, Jr., "Memphis and the Quantum Leap," *Memphis* 1 (July 1970), 27–33; Judith A. Moncrieff, "Greater Memphis Plans Development," *National Civic Review* 58 (Oct. 1969), 437–38.

3. *Commercial Appeal,* Sept. 22, 1970.

sulted by the white business elite. Banker Lewis McKee voiced these new concerns to the news media when he declared: "working for better educational and job opportunities for Negroes has a high priority in our program. . . . We are proving to those who decide to locate manufacturing plants, home offices and distribution centers here that they will not have to concern themselves with the race problem in Memphis because we're 'on top of it' and making good progress towards its solution."[4]

When the NAACP organized a student boycott of the public schools in the fall of 1969, seeking to enforce demands for black representation on the all-white school board and for the hiring of more black teachers and administrators, the chamber of commerce provided leadership that settled the "Black Monday" boycotts, demonstrations, and vandalism. Bankers and moderate NAACP leaders negotiated a settlement in which blacks agreed to a boycott moratorium and the business leaders promised to persuade the school board to accept two black advisers, Dr. Hollis Price and George Brown, and to secure legislation changing the selection of school board members from at-large to district elections, thus permitting blacks to win seats on the board of education.[5]

When federal judge Robert M. McRae, Jr. finally told Memphis school officials in April 1972 that they would have to bus white students, the chamber of commerce again took the lead in accepting change. The business leaders did not believe in busing, but they did believe in public tranquillity and the national reputation of Memphis. So the chamber quietly organized IMPACT (Involved Memphis Parents Assisting Children and Teachers), a public relations campaign of television advertising, public speakers, and neighborhood meetings to preserve the public schools. IMPACT never defended busing because, as a chamber spokesman said, "we couldn't. . . . What we defended was abiding by the law, and preserving public education in this city, this country. Public education has to be

4. "Wide-Awake Down South," *Nation's Business* (Feb. 1971), 55; Barney Du-Bois, "The Power Structure," *Commercial Appeal*, Sept. 20, 1970.

5. *Ibid.; Tri-State Defender,* Oct. 4, 25, Nov. 8, 23, 1969; *Memphis Press-Scimitar,* Nov. 14, 1969; Mrs. Frances Coe to author, Aug. 5, 1974.

salvaged—it's vital, essential. Without it, all our major institutions are threatened. So we have to change."[6]

IMPACT failed to prevent a white flight from public education. Before court-ordered busing, 45 percent of the students were white, but almost half of them fled to private schools, making blacks almost 70 percent of the remaining public school population. While IMPACT failed to prevent the flourishing of church-sponsored private schools, its propaganda efforts probably assisted in preserving public order. Schoolbuses encountered no violence, and even the head of Citizens Against Busing, Ken Keele, who had brandished a two-by-four and threatened to stop buses from rolling, reported to the police a white man who offered to dynamite the buses.[7]

The chamber of commerce clearly emerged as the most prominent organization in Memphis after 1968, putting out racial fires and promoting harmony. The business leaders raised four million dollars over the next three years to "keep the town from blowing up." But the 1973 recession then injured local industrial leaders, and several withdrew from civic leadership. Small business members of the chamber had always opposed the social programs. As the chamber of commerce lost members, it fell into debt and abandoned its community goals.[8]

Even as the recession of 1973 began, the chamber shifted back to rhetoric with the Believe in Memphis Program. This splendid public relations campaign to sell Memphians on their own city was headed by Wallace E. Johnson, one of the greatest "believers" of all time. Johnson was a Mississippi-born carpenter who, with Kemmons Wilson, had moved from housing construction to organizing the largest motel chain in the world, Holiday Inns. Johnson proudly related his personal belief. In 1948 he offered a typical prayer:

> O Lord, make us one of the greatest leaders of the nation in the building of men and homes, and help the city officials of Memphis to understand that this is our goal, so they will help us instead of hinder

6. John Egerton, *Promise of Progress: Memphis School Desegregation 1972–1973* (Atlanta: Southern Regional Council, 1973), 8.

7. *Ibid.*, 12; *Commercial Appeal*, Aug. 28, 1973; *Wall Street Journal*, Dec. 17, 1973.

8. *Commercial Appeal*, Sept. 11, 1977.

us. Make me, O Lord, one of the leading Baptists and teach me how to win souls. O Lord, help me to be one of the biggest businessmen in the United States, and if it be Thy Will, let me be vice-president of the National Home Builders' Association.

God, please, oh, please, let us build two thousand units this year, and if it be in accordance with Thy divine purpose, let us accumulate $250,000 in cash during that time. O Lord, help us to build a good house cheaper than anyone else in the United States. Help us to get lumber, or sawmills, or whatever else we need. May we be able to house the Negro citizens of our community as they have never been housed before. And, God, please, oh, please help us to make connection with the right kind of banks, that understand that mortgages on Negro property are as safe an investment as any other kind, so that we can go on and on and on. Amen.[9]

Johnson had achieved all that he had asked and therefore was the ideal man to tell Memphians they could do the same. He launched his Believe in Memphis Program by inviting another of America's leading positive thinkers, Reverend Norman Vincent Peale, to tell the local chamber of commerce:

Memphis's greatest assets are its problems. Problems constitute a sign of life. They are a device by which communities grow strong.

We grow mentally and spiritually as we tussle with our problems.

Believe in Memphis: believe in yourself; believe in God; believe in your country; believe in people; believe in the future!

If you believe in Memphis and talk it up and work it up, a greater Memphis will flow back to you.[10]

Wallace Johnson continued with a massive propaganda effort that he intended to drown out all the "poor-mouthing" of "one of America's loveliest cities." His campaign and that of the chamber of commerce campaign launched a complete public relations program with radio and television spot commercials boasting of the city's heritage: "Memphis is . . . the city that gave birth to the Blues, the Memphis Sound, and the Cotton Carnival, . . . home of the South's

9. Charles Sopkin (ed.) "The Millionaire: A Self-Portrait," *Esquire* (Feb. 1964), 92-93; Wallace E. Johnson, "Why I Pray to Succeed," *Guideposts* (April 1967), 12-15; Wallace E. Johnson, *Work is My Play* (New York: Hawthorn, 1973); John Joseph Pepin, "An Investigation of the Key Strategic Decisions in the Development of Holiday Inns of America, Inc." (Ph.D. diss., Univ. of Mississippi, 1969).

10. *Commercial Appeal,* Jan. 26, 1973.

first blood bank, the world's first self-service supermarket, the country's first motor vehicle inspection bureau, . . . the only city ever to have the nation's Cleanest City Award four times. . . . " There were "Memphis Believer" bumper stickers and decals. There were pledge cards: "Yes, I am a Memphis Believer and want to help in the Believe in Memphis Program." There were even educational seminars to instruct taxi drivers, waitresses, hotel clerks, and service station attendants to "talk up" Memphis.[11]

The concern with talking up Memphis distinguished the chamber leadership from the old reformers who had pursued problems without resorting to civic boosterism. The chamber's Believe in Memphis campaign may have deemphasized racial division within the city, although certainly black-white division persisted, but surely the media advertising reminds us that a chamber of commerce is not primarily a reform organization. A commercial organization is concerned primarily with economic growth, while reformers attempt to repair and maintain liberal democracy. Chamber of commerce interest in blacks emerged from the search for a proper advertising image to attract Northern industry; reformer concern for blacks reflected their belief that democracy should work in Memphis.

The chamber never even attempted to perpetuate the civic reformer practice of persuading good men to run for local office. Not even the business elite took much interest in "good government" candidates, although a general decline in quality was acknowledged. Memphis business executives had organized their own civic group in 1961, Future Memphis, Inc. With membership limited to the top 100 executives in local business, the exclusive group operated quietly without publicity, keeping all actions confidential but somehow still encouraging projects such as running an interstate expressway through the city's major green space, Overton Park, consolidation of city and county government, constructing a convention center, and celebrating the Memphis Sesquicentennial.[12] Future Memphis, with its managerial exclusiveness, its good fellowship, and its quiet boosting of a greater Memphis, certainly demonstrated

11. *Ibid.,* Nov. 22, 1972.
12. Future Memphis Inc., "History of Future Memphis Inc." (Memphis: Future Memphis, 1974) Mimeographed.

that a civic organization could survive. But passionate Memphis reformers never approved of the avoidance of politics characteristic of Future Memphis and its exclusion of editor Edward Meeman from membership while it elected instead a business manager of Memphis Publishing Company who handled the financial details of Meeman's newspaper.

Unlike Future Memphis, Meeman, Orgill, and Burch had been more concerned with enacting democratic ideas than securing social pleasure, and had eagerly included women, labor, blacks, and anyone else interested in working for good government. Passion for democratic success had led the reformers to move beyond discussion into political action. Urged on by Edward Meeman, the agitator of the group, they had gone into politics to elect a liberal democrat, Estes Kefauver, and to enact reform ideas. Meeman delighted in saying, "Citizens working alone can do much. A newspaper working alone can do much. But citizens working with their newspaper can do anything." He pursued good government even beyond his death in 1966, leaving his entire estate of two million dollars in the Edward J. Meeman Foundation for the promotion of democracy, good journalism, and the conservation of natural resources.[13] But the Meeman Foundation money could never replace that enthusiasm earlier promoted by Memphis's most zealous good government reformer.

Edmund Orgill, earnest leader of the civic reformers, remained active through 1968. After retiring as mayor he continued as a leader of the Citizens Association and its campaign for metropolitan consolidation; he served on a citizens committee that advised the city commission to purchase the local bus system in 1960; he joined the Memphis Light, Gas, and Water Commission to lead Memphis back into the Tennessee Valley Authority system; and he won election to the Shelby County Quarterly Court in 1966 to promote reapportionment. He was a director of the Memphis Urban League and the local War on Poverty Committee, and chairman of

13. Edward J. Meeman Foundation Declaration in Trust, Meeman Papers; the trustees, headed by Edmund Orgill and Lucius Burch, quickly divided most of the money among Memphis State University, Southwestern, LeMoyne-Owen, and the University of Tennessee.

the Memphis Committee on Community Relations.[14] But by 1968 illness was forcing Orgill to relinquish both his political and civic leadership. No one stepped forward to replace the individual who had been the sustaining force in the reform organizations. Twenty years earlier the repression of local democracy had produced Orgill and the other volunteer reformers, but now the free political system seemed to produce citizen disinterest in elections, public opposition to the social scientist solutions for urban ills, and racial division of the community.

The black and the Republican revolutions had surely soured bi-racial and bipartisan cooperation. Not even the extreme civic distress associated with the sanitation strike could restore bi-racial cooperation. Lucius Burch, the liberal sparkplug for the civic reformers, tired of criticism from conservative whites and militant blacks and turned to a more successful crusade for converting the old Shelby County Penal Farm on the eastern edge of the city into a public park. So the civic reform era ended in 1968, two decades after it had begun. Except for the chamber of commerce's new concern for racial harmony, only the quiet breakfasts arranged by Ben Hooks and Jed Dreifuss grew out of the King assassination. Every month a few individuals from both communities met to talk with each other and the media leaders at the Little Tea Shop in downtown Memphis. Until racial and political hostilities mellowed, civic reform would surely consist only of tearoom communication and campaigns by the chamber of commerce.[15]

In Overton Park a bronze statue of Boss Crump reminds Memphians of their admiration for a leader who appealed to their baser instincts—fear, parsimony, and vanity—but no civic honor paid tribute to those who had asked for ideals such as generosity, understanding, the brotherhood of man, and the solutions of urban theorists. The reformers, it would seem, had never really succeeded. They never persuaded Memphians to turn Boss Crump from power nor had they prevented the divisive Henry Loeb, whose appeals

14. *Commercial Appeal,* July 15, 1966.
15. *Commercial Appeal,* Feb. 27, 1974; Thomas BeVier, "Getting the Most out of the Buffalo's Snort," *Mid-South Magazine,* July 14, 1974, 15–23; *Memphis Press-Scimitar,* Jan. 21, 1975.

were much the same as Crump's, from attaining office. They never convinced Memphians to try the city manager form of government. Their plans for city-county consolidation were repeatedly rejected by the voters. And most distressing of all, black leaders moved beyond white liberal support of desegregation to demand busing, racial quotas, and 40 percent of Memphis. By the seventies even their two liberal senators, Ested Kefauver and Albert Gore, had been replaced by more conservative Republicans. So despite their restoration of democracy in Memphis and their other good works, the Memphis reformers seemed destined to be remembered, if at all, only in a history book.

The thousands of hours and dollars invested in their arduous quest had not created a reformed community. As Lucius Burch admitted, "the liberal causes in which I have personally been most concerned and active have failed."[16] Their toils produced precious little success; they wished they could have accomplished more. But still the effort seemed worth the cost. As Burch assured Edmund Orgill back in 1948, even though they failed they could take pride in their struggle, recalling "what I aspired to be, and was not, comforts me." Even as they candidly admitted failure, little glimmers of pride seemed to show through when they talked of having had the courage to stand up against a petty local tyrant, the determination to bring professional planners into city government, and the wisdom to prevent a Little Rock or Birmingham style racial disorder while their mayor controlled city hall.

If machine government were to return to Memphis the reformers would surely regard this as the most distressing failure of all. They believed, as did all good government men, that bosses and machines were relics of the past which, if eliminated, would never return. The reformers knew nothing of the predictions of the political scientists that the big cities would likely return to machine rule as whites fled to the suburbs leaving black and Spanish-speaking people to restore power to a friendly boss.[17] Memphis might someday have a black boss who, like Crump, would pacify the masses with personal atten-

16. Burch, "Why I am a Liberal," 25-33.
17. Milton L. Rakove, *Don't Make No Waves: Don't Back No Losers* (Bloomington: Indiana Univ. Press, 1975), 18-19, 277.

tion and municipal services, moderate racial conflict, and perhaps even hold down taxes. Although the central city elected a black congressman, Harold Ford, in 1972, Memphis remained 60 percent white and free to expand its boundaries by annexation. So long as the city continued to annex fleeing white suburbanites back into Memphis, the black population and any political machine would surely fall short of a voting majority. For some time to come, it appeared, Memphis would drift free of control from either civic reformers or machine government.

Essay on Sources

Edmund Orgill made this book possible by opening his own private papers and also the papers of E. J. Meeman, the Civic Research Committee, and the Citizens Association, all of which are now available in the Mississippi Valley Collection, Brister Library, Memphis State University, which has virtually all of the manuscript collections for recent Memphis history.

The Edmund Orgill Papers (1940-1972)—thirty-eight large boxes and thirty-eight scrapbooks—offer complete records on the mayor's administration as well as correspondence on the Atlantic Union, Estes Kefauver, Civic Research, MCCR, Citizens Association, Memphis Light, Gas, and Water Division, War on Poverty Committee, metropolitan consolidation, and the Metropolitan Inter-Faith Association.

The Edward J. Meeman Papers (1889-1962)—thirteen boxes—include an unpublished autobiography as well as correspondence concerning Christian Science, moral rearmament, journalism, parks and conservation, Civic Research, MCCR, E. H. Crump, Lucius Burch, Jr., and Estes Kefauver.

The Civic Research Committee Papers (1949-1961)—fifteen boxes—are especially complete because the executive secretary, Charles Pool, was a historian concerned with preserving an adequate record. The correspondence, membership, reports, reference, and newspaper clipping files are excellent until 1959, when Pool resigned, and then the papers fail to tell the story of the organization's decline.

The Citizens Association Papers (1959-1967)—eleven boxes—are thin on correspondence but strong on the files of ward and precinct organizations as well as membership lists and minutes of meetings.

The Watkins Overton Papers (1894-1958)—fourteen boxes—are the best available look inside Crump's organization. The papers of E. H. Crump himself have been tightly retained by the family and no other prominent Crumpite has made his records publicly available except Senator K. D. Mc-Kellar, whose papers are in the Memphis-Shelby County Public Library. The Crump-McKellar correspondence has been conveniently boxed together.

The M. A. Hinds Papers (1928-1965)—thirty-two boxes and forty-two scrapbooks—date mostly from 1959, when he became sheriff and began planning to become mayor. This anti-reformer kept files on every local political figure and public issue from the years 1959-1964. Some of the material goes back to Hind's earlier career as a city policeman during Crump's day.

The George Grider Papers (1964-1966)—forty-three boxes—relate entirely to his two political campaigns and his congressional work, but are valuable for understanding the reformers' loss of political power in Memphis. The Dan Kuykendall Papers (1966-1974) are also in the Mississippi Valley Collection but are closed to scholars until 1985.

The Arthur W. McCain Papers (1961-1968) consist of only one box but are an important source for understanding the work of the MCCR and for copies of local NAACP reports.

The Program for Progress Papers (1966)—seven file boxes—contain committee correspondence, minutes of all meetings, newspaper clippings, and a manuscript history of the change in government written by Jack Morris.

Interviews are an important source for understanding recent history, and Brister Library has two tape transcript collections. The Oral History Research Project has three transcripts of value—transcripts of interviews with Frank Ahlgren, Frances E. Coe and George W. Lee—and the Sanitation Strike Archives has more than a hundred, including transcripts of talks with most of the Memphians prominent in politics and civil rights during the sixties. While the author profited from these interviews, he preferred the less complicated pen and notebook for his own interviews and made no tapes.

The Memphis and Shelby County Archives, Memphis-Shelby County Public Library, has the papers of several mayors (1940-1954) during Crump's years in power. Beginning with Walter Chandler and continuing through Sylvanus Polk, James J. Pleasants, and Frank Tobey, the mayors left their correspondence with the city archives. Thereafter the mayors took their files when they left office, except for Henry Loeb, and his papers were opened after this manuscript was completed.

No papers of black Memphians are available except for those of George W. Lee, which are now in the Amistad Research Center, Dillard University. Lee's papers consist largely of newspaper clippings and Republican correspondence. The papers of Lee's mentor and of Memphis's most distinguished black family, the Robert R. Churches, have recently been donated to Memphis State University's Mississippi Valley Collection; most of these documents have been published in Church, *The Robert R. Churches of Memphis.*

The single biography of Crump—Miller, *Mr. Crump of Memphis*—a work approved and subsidized by Crump's family, remains largely unchallenged because no other scholar has had access to the papers. To balance the biography of the "honest boss," one can read parts of older works such as Key, Perry, Capers ("Memphis"), and McIlwaine.

There is no published study of the *Memphis Press-Scimitar.* Baker, *The Memphis Commercial Appeal* is very thin on the last three decades and less critical than the journalism monthly *More* (May 1974), which voted the paper one of America's ten worst daily newspapers.

The Egyptians (1914–) should be consulted by anyone interested in Memphis history. The papers read before this exclusive group are available only at Southwestern University at Memphis.

Books

Bartholomew, Harland and Associates. *Comprehensive Plan: Memphis, Tenn.* St. Louis, Mo.: HBA, 1955.

Bishop, Jim. *The Days of Martin Luther King Jr.* New York: Putnam's, 1971.

Bunche, Ralph J. *The Political Status of the Negro in the Age of F.D.R.* Ed. Dewey W. Grantham. Chicago: Univ. of Chicago Press, 1973.

Capers, Gerald. *The Biography of a River Town: Memphis, Its Heroic Age.* Chapel Hill: Univ. of North Carolina Press, 1939.

Cartwright, Joseph H. *The Triumph of Jim Crow: Tennessee Race Relations in the 1880s.* Knoxville: Univ. of Tenn. Press, 1976.

Catledge, Turner. *My Life and The Times.* New York: Harper, 1971.

Church, Annette E. and Roberta. *The Robert R. Churches of Memphis.* Ann Arbor: Edwards Bros., 1974.

Duster, Alfreda M. (ed.) *Crusader for Justice: The Autobiography of Ida B. Wells.* Chicago: Univ. of Chicago Press, 1970.

Egerton, John. *Promise of Progress: Memphis School Desegregation 1972–1973.* Atlanta, Ga.: Southern Regional Council, 1973.

Frank, Gerold. *An American Death.* Garden City, N.Y.: Doubleday, 1972.

Gorman, Joseph Bruce. *Kefauver: A Political Biography.* New York: Oxford Univ. Press, 1971.

Graham, Hugh Davis. *Crisis in Print: Desegregation and the Press in Tennessee.* Nashville: Vanderbilt Univ. Press, 1967.

Grider, George and Lydel Sims. *War Fish.* Boston: Little, Brown, 1958.

Hamilton, G.P. *The Bright Side of Memphis.* Memphis: G.P. Hamilton, 1908.

Jackson, Kenneth T. *The Ku Klux Klan in the City 1915-1930*. New York: Oxford Univ. Press, 1967.

Johnson, Wallace E. *Work is My Play*. New York: Hawthorn, 1973.

Key, V. O. *Southern Politics in State and Nation*. New York: Knopf, 1949.

Lamon, Lester C. *Black Tennesseans 1900-1930*. Knoxville: Univ. of Tennessee Press, 1977.

Lee, George W. *Beale Street: Where the Blues Began*. New York: Ballou, 1934.

Lewis, David L. *King: A Critical Biography*. Baltimore: Penguin, 1970.

Mason, Lucy Randolph. *To Win These Rights: A Personal History of the CIO in the South*. New York: Harper, 1952.

McIlwaine, Shields. *Memphis Down in Dixie*. New York: Dutton, 1948.

Meeman, Edward J. *The Editorial We: A Posthumous Autobiography*. Ed. Edwin Howard. Memphis: Memphis State Univ. Printing Services, 1976.

Merrill, Bergen S., Jr. (ed.) *Memphis in the Seventies*. Memphis: Memphis State Univ. Press, 1970.

Miller, William D. *Memphis During the Progressive Era*. Memphis: Memphis State Univ. Press, 1957.

_____. *Mr. Crump of Memphis*. Baton Rouge, La.: Louisiana State Univ. Press, 1964.

Muse, Benjamin. *Memphis*. Atlanta, Ga.: Southern Regional Council, 1964.

Perry, Jennings. *Democracy Begins at Home: The Tennessee Fight for the Poll Tax*. Philadelphia: Lippincott, 1944.

Peterson, Lorin. *The Day of the Mugwump*. New York: Random, 1961.

Purcell, Theodore V. and Gerald F. Cavanaugh, *Blacks in the Industrial World*. New York: Free Press, 1972.

Rakove, Milton L. *Don't Make No Waves: Don't Back No Losers*. Bloomington: Indiana Univ. Press, 1975.

Riggs, Joseph H. (ed.) *Gordon Browning: An Oral Memoir*. Memphis: Memphis Public Library, 1966.

Smith, Frank E. *Congressman from Mississippi*. New York: Pantheon, 1964.

Stanfield, J. Edwin, *In Memphis: More than a Garbage Strike*. Atlanta, Ga.: Southern Regional Council, 1968.

Streit, Clarence K. *Union Now: The Proposal for Inter-Democracy Federal Union*. New York: Harper, 1940.

Tucker, David M. *Black Pastors and Leaders*. Memphis: Memphis State Univ. Press, 1975.

_____. *Lieutenant Lee of Beale Street*. Nashville: Vanderbilt Univ. Press, 1971.

U.S. Commission on Civil Rights, *Employment, Administration of Justice and Health Services in Memphis-Shelby County, Tenn.* Washington, D.C.: GPO, 1967.

_____. *Hearings Before the U.S. Commission in Civil Rights, Memphis, June, 1962.* Washington: GPO, 1963.

U.S. Bureau of the Census. *Negroes in the United States 1920–1930.* Washington, D.C. GPO, 1935.

Wildavsky, Aaron. *Dixon-Yates: A Study in Power Politics.* New Haven: Yale Univ. Press, 1962.

Wright, William E. *Memphis Politics: A Study in Bloc Voting.* New York: McGraw-Hill, 1962.

Articles

Bridges, Lamar Whitlow. "Editor Mooney Versus Boss Crump." *West Ten-Tennessee Historical Society Papers* 20 (1966), 77–107.

Burch, Lucius E., Jr. "Characteristics of the American Negro." *The Egyptians* (1948), 49–57.

_____. "Plans for Peace." *The Egyptians* (1948), 198–213.

_____. "Council-Manager Government as Related to Memphis, Tennessee." *The Egyptians* (1951), 49–59.

_____. "Why I am a Liberal." *The Egyptians* (1975), 25–33.

Capers, Gerald. "Memphis, Satrapy of a Benevolent Despot." In *Our Fair City.* Ed. Robert S. Allen. New York: Vanguard, 1947.

Collins, Thomas W. "Unionization in a Secondary Labor Market." *Human Organization* 36 (Summer 1977), 135–41.

Gotten, Henry B. "Mud, Mules and Molasses." *The Egyptians* (1967), 51–71.

Greene, Lee S., and Jack E. Holmes. "Tennessee: A Politics of Peaceful Change." In *The Changing Politics of the South.* Ed. William C. Havard. Baton Rouge: Louisiana State Univ. Press, 1972.

Haas, Edward F. "The Southern Metropolis, 1940–1976." In *The City in Southern History.* Ed. Blaine A. Brownell and David R. Goldfield. Port Washington, N.Y.: Kennikat, 1977.

Kitchens, Allen H. "Ouster of Mayor Edward H. Crump 1915–1916." *West Tennessee Historical Society Papers* 19 (1965), 105–20.

Majors, William R. "Gordon Browning and Tennessee Politics, 1937–1953." *Tennessee Historical Quarterly* 28 (Spring 1969), 57–69, and part 2 (Summer 1969), 166–81.

Marshall, F. Ray and Arvil Van Adams. "Negro Employment in Memphis." *Industrial Relations: A Journal of Economy and Society* 9 (May 1970), 308–23.

Porteous, Clark. "Memphis Politics—Past and Present." *The Egyptians* (1963), 45–67.

Rickey, Albert C. "City County Consolidation: The Inside Story." *The Egyptians* (1972), 1–15.

Streit, Clarence K. "Two Eds that Think as One." *Freedom and Union* 21 (Feb. 1966), 3-5.
Sugg, Redding S., Jr. "Memphis and the Quantum Leap." *Memphis* 1 (July 1970), 27-33.
Tucker, David M. "Miss Ida B. Wells and Memphis Lynching." *Phylon* 32 (Summer 1971), 112-22.
_____. "Black Politics in Memphis 1865-1875" *West Tennessee Historical Society Papers* 26 (1972), 13-19.

Theses

Adkins, Walter P. "Beale Street Goes to the Polls." M.A. thesis, Ohio State Univ., 1935.
Leake, George Craig. "A Presentation of the Script and Production Background for the Television Documentary 'The Once and Always Mister Crump.'" M.A. thesis, Memphis State Univ., 1968.
Pepin, John Joseph. "An Investigation of the Key Strategic Decisions in the Development of Holiday Inns of America, Inc." Ph.D. diss., Univ. of Mississippi, 1969.
Phillips, Virginia M. "Rowlett Paine's First Term as Mayor of Memphis 1920-1924." M.A. thesis, Memphis State Univ., 1958.
Ruden, Paul M. "Transitional Politics: The Development of a Two-Party System in Memphis and Shelby County, Tennessee." Senior thesis, Yale Univ., 1964.
Wax, Jonathan I. "Program of Progress, A Step Into the Present." Senior thesis, Princeton Univ., 1968.

Index

Agrarians, 34, 41
Ahlgren, Frank, 74–75, 84–85, 96, 102, 112–13, 137, 156
Allen Steam Plant, 90, 90–91n
American Federation of Labor, 15, 32, 56, 58, 63, 152–60
Annexation, 69, 91, 101, 172
Apperson, John, 44
Armour, Claude A., 81, 85, 86, 87, 102, 136–37, 140
Armstrong, Walter Jr., 107, 115
Awsumb, Gwen, 77, 114, 158–59

Bailey, Walter, 137–38
Barr, William M., 49–50, 71, 100
Barret, Paul W., 108
Bartholomew, Harland, 70, 81, 91–92, 95
Bates, Bert, 70
Beale Street, 14
Believe in Memphis Program, 166–68
Binford, Lloyd T., 75–76
Bisso, Louis, 70
Black Memphians: reconstruction politics, 3–6; lynching, 6–14; business, 14–16; machine politics, 16–21; coalition with reformers, 56–58, 64–65, 76–77, 82–85, 88–89; poverty

Black Memphians (*cont.*)
and housing, 93; campaign for office, 101–102, 141–42; push desegregation, 118–42; unite behind sanitation strike, 152–61; elect a congressman, 172
Black Monday, 165
Blanchard, Jerred, 157–58
Boyle, Joe, 19, 30
Bratton, O.D., 52, 64
Brewster, W. Herbert, 155
Brown, Bailey, 61
Brown, C. Whitney, 115
Brown, George, 165
Brown, Palmer III, 109–10
Browning, Gordon, 29–30, 59, 65
Bruce, C. Arthur, 148
Buchignani, Leo, 144
Buckman, Stanley J., 100, 102, 107, 109
Burch, Lucius E. Jr.: young liberal, 41–42, 44; draws Orgill into politics, 45–48, 50–51, 58, 60; civic reformer, 62–64, 66–67, 87, 98, 100, 103, 108; pushes for new charter, 112–13, 115–16; leads MCCR, 120–22, 133, 134–35, 136, 141; rejects racial quotas, 163; turns to Shelby

179

Index

THE UNIVERSITY OF TENNESSEE PRESS
KNOXVILLE